How to Build a Snowman and Other Stories

Growing Up in a Northern Mill Town in the 1960s and 1970s

by
Howard Thorp

Published by New Generation Publishing in 2024

Copyright © Howard Thorp 2024

First Edition

The author asserts the moral right under the Copyright, Designs and Patents Act 1988 to be identified as the author of this work.

All Rights reserved. No part of this publication may be reproduced, stored in a retrieval system or transmitted, in any form or by any means without the prior consent of the author, nor be otherwise circulated in any form of binding or cover other than that which it is published and without a similar condition being imposed on the subsequent purchaser.

ISBN   978-1-83563-126-3

www.newgeneration-publishing.com

New Generation Publishing

*For my mother and father Mavis and Geoff
and in memory of my friend David Fletcher*

CONTENTS

PROLOGUE vii
Chapter 1: IN THE BEGINNING 1
Chapter 2: AND IN THE PAST... 11
Chapter 3: EARLY DAYS 17
Chapter 4: FAMILY LIFE... 25
Chapter 5: JUNIOR SCHOOL 43
Chapter 6: FREEZING WINTERS AND LONG HOT SUMMERS 49
Chapter 7: CULTURE 57
Chapter 8: GRAMMAR SCHOOL... 71
Chapter 9: TEENAGE ANGST 95
Chapter 10: AFTERWORD.. 121

PROLOGUE

They say you know when you are getting old when you look in the mirror and see wrinkles, a receding hairline, or grey hair, but what really brings it home to you is when you look back on your childhood from middle age and realise you lived in a world which was very different from the world today. As L P Hartley famously said in the Go Between – "The past is a foreign country: they do things differently there". I was born 12 years after the end of the Second World War into a Northern England, which still lay in the shadow of it. When I was a lad, the world was a curious mixture of old and new – the dawn of the space age and the decaying remnants of Victorian industrial muscle and civic splendour.

In the North where I grew up, many people still lived in back-to-back terrace houses which had coal fires, an outside privy in the backyard, and a front door which opened right onto the street. There were still steam trains running on British Railways, and very few people went on foreign holidays, or had ever been abroad. Many people didn't have cars. Now, those houses have been modernised and have central heating and indoor toilets and bathrooms; British Rail and steam trains have gone, and foreign holidays are the norm.

The overall physical landscape of the urban and suburban Manchester area where I grew up appears not to have changed greatly since then[1]; when you look more closely, there have been remarkable changes. In the 50s and 60s, the horizons around Manchester were still dominated by mill chimneys and there were no great orbital motorways. The clean air acts of the 1950s created to smokeless zones; although we had a coal fire, we used smokeless fuel, and this led to a vast improvement in the urban atmosphere. The great and deadly smogs of the 50s became a thing of the past. Despite this, the large public buildings in town centres, such as Manchester Town Hall and the Royal Exchange, were still covered black with soot, the mark of the industrial revolution.

---

[1] It hadn't when I originally wrote this, but it has now - in the 21st century. Manchester now has a skyline full of towers.

My maternal Grandmother, Annie Thomas, was born in 1900, at a time when horse-drawn transport was the norm, coal and steam were the main sources of power, and many people still worked as servants for the better off. My paternal Grandfather James Thorp, born in 1897, fought in the infantry in the first World War a time when many perished. Both of them lived through two World Wars and endured great hardship, which is difficult to relate to today.

By the late 1940s, for ordinary people, many things, which we now take for granted, were only available to the wealthy or the relatively small middle class of professionals. Many people did not have bank accounts; there were no credit cards; money was in pounds, shillings, and pence as it had been for centuries past, including tanners[2] and threepenny bits; many people did not have a car or a phone in the house; TV was black and white with only two channels; and gas central heating and computers were unheard of. Postwar Britain was a time of great change, and by the 1950s, Britain was beginning to become more prosperous. New homes and council houses were replacing the back-to-back terraces. Central heating and telephones were being installed in many houses, and more people were able to afford to own cars.

According to Phillip Larkin[3]:

"Sexual intercourse began
In nineteen sixty three
(Which was rather late for me) –
Between the end of the Chatterley ban
And the Beatles first LP."

Larkin was slightly late because many of the changes which were really felt, or acknowledged, to belong to the 60s, such as greater sexual openness, had really begun in the 50s. The 50s was a world of nuclear power, the beginnings of space exploration, 'Angry Young Men', mutual assured destruction, Suez and end of Empire, of Miles Davis, Charlie Parker, the Beat Poets, Rock n' Roll, and the gadgetry

---

[2] A sixpenny bit.
[3] From 'Annus Mirabilis' in High Windows published by Faber & Faber 1974.

of James Bond. We like to think of the world in decades because it's convenient but society's development doesn't neatly respect the calendar.

The period of optimism and enlightenment we think of as the "swinging sixties" started in the 50s with the postwar economic boom in America, and Rock and Roll, the end of 13 years of Tory government, and ended with Sergeant Peppers, the 'revolutions' of 1968, and the Moon landing in 1969. Then, in the early 1970s, there began a period of decline and disillusionment, industrial action, an oil crisis, and rampant inflation. In popular music, there was a period of over-elaboration and excess with progressive rock, and the highs of the 60s music and fashion with icons like Mary Quant ended in the 'hangover' of Thatcher and the winter of discontent. Punk Rock was the turning point, a prophetic sign of things to come.

Then we had a long dark period of reaction with mass unemployment, the Falklands War, the Miner's Strike, privatisation, and Tory government working for the rich. That period should have ended in 1992 but was curiously extended by the Major government in an election the Tories ought to have lost. Now, we are in an intermediate phase, well below the heights (and highs) of the "Sixties", a slight improvement on the Thatcher nightmare but a continuation of Thatcher's disastrous anti-worker policies from a Blairite government[4].

So, just 6 months after I was born, on 20 July 1957, Harold Macmillan told an audience of Tories "Let's be frank about it; most of our people have never had it so good. Go around the country, go to the industrial towns, go to the farms, and you will see a state of prosperity such as we have never had in my lifetime − nor indeed in the history of this country". People had rejected the postwar austerity and rationing that had come with the Atlee government and were desperate to modernise and escape from material hardships.

The era of the Beatles and Harold Wilson's "white heat of technology" of the contraceptive pill, Carnaby Street, the expansion of universities, men on the moon, the Abortion Act, the common use of cannabis and other recreational drugs, and homosexual law reform was waiting for me just around the corner............ let the story begin!

---

[4] I wrote this before the horrors of thirteen years of Tory government we are now enduring.

MAP OF ALKRINGTON

This is a map I drew of Alkrington, where I grew up and lived from 1960 to 1975. We lived at no 86, Warwick Road.

Note: Nearly all of the photographs in this book were taken by my father Geoffrey Alan Thorp. There are a few exceptions where I have been unable to identify the photographer, but I am more than happy to give credit if they contact me.

Chapter 1
IN THE BEGINNING

I was born in Sale, near Manchester, on the 23 January 1957, at Sale Cottage Hospital. I guess that means I was born at the start of the space age, though it hardly felt like it in the North of England. I can't remember many details about the first few years of my life, but the country was still very grey in that postwar time. It was almost like living in a black and white movie, like those classic films Look Back in Anger, This Sporting Life, and Saturday Night and Sunday Morning.

There were dark coats, black cars, and terraced streets with smoking chimneys, great mills with tall mill chimneys, and seemingly endless Tory Government. When you went for a trip into Manchester, many of the large buildings, including the Town Hall and Central Reference Library, were still blackened with soot. There were also some plots of derelict land, which were a legacy from bombing in the Second World War. It seemed almost as if colour hadn't been invented until the 60s started.

Looking back, the postwar era might appear to be grey and bleak, but that would be very misleading, for this was also a time of increasing prosperity bursting with invention and energy. Watson and Crick discovered the double-helix structure of the DNA molecule. Sellafield nuclear power station began generating energy in 1956. It was also the age of the teenager and increasing optimism about the future. We had great music with rock n' roll, Elvis Presley, Buddy Holly, and brilliant jazz musicians like Miles Davis[5] and John Coltrane, painters like Jackson Pollock, writers such as Jack Kerouac[6], and the beat poets including Allen Ginsberg and Lawrence Ferlinghetti. It was a time when things, like Sputnik, were taking off!

My earliest memories must relate to when I lived with my parents in a rented house on Urban Road in Sale. Good street name that, sums up my origins nicely. The memories are vague, but I can

---

[5] My favourite is the album Kind of Blue which is still rated highly one of the best albums of all time.
[6] His great book was On The Road. I recommend the book and the film.

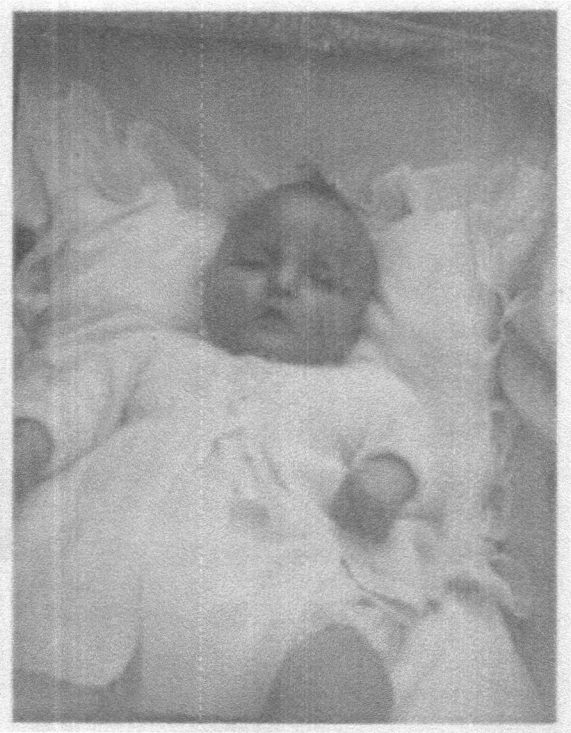

Baby Howard

recall playing with friends, living near a railway line with real steam trains! and the local shops. The Manchester tram network now runs on that same line. Of course, I can remember my parents too. Both of them were born in the mid 1930s and had grown up in the Second World War. I remember my Dad, Geoffrey, telling me stories about the hardships, mainly centred around food rationing, the delights of powdered egg, the lack of chocolate, and the blackout.

Dad was born in October 1935 and only 4 years old when WWII started. All of us who are children of parents of that generation will be familiar with "turn that light off!" They had lived through a time of war and the blackout. One of my Dad's favourite sayings was "It's like Blackpool illuminations in this house!" as he went round turning the lights off. Many others he used were classics of his time – "Put wood in t'hole!" (shut the door!), "Pull your socks up", "Grin and bear it", "You're as daft as a brush", "What did your last slave die of", "I want never gets", "Marry in haste, repent at leisure", "and "Give us a shufti" (meaning a quick look at something).

My Mum and Dad were fairly young as parents tended to be in those days. I know my Dad was 21 when I was born. He wore glasses, had short brown hair, liked jazz, and loved cycling. He was also a keen photographer and gardener. In the 1950s, he played the washboard in a skiffle group. He was brought up a Catholic but lapsed when he was in his teens. He worked as a lab technician for ICI in Rhodes[7] after leaving Sale Grammar school when he was 14 years old because his family couldn't afford for him to stay at school. It was a tragedy for him because he would have gone on to university, something he always regretted missing out on. Later in life, he went to night school at Manchester College of Technology[8] for several years and got a diploma in chemical engineering – equivalent to a pass degree. He started work at ICI and went on to work for the Clayton Aniline Company, making dyestuffs. The company was later taken over by Ciba Geigy and at the time was the largest factory in Manchester.

My Dad on the far right with colleagues at Clayton Aniline company

---

[7] Rhodes in Lancashire – or now Greater Manchester.
[8] Later UMIST and now part of Manchester University.

My Mum, Mavis, was born in 1934, had long brown hair, was pretty, and liked music, sketching, and ice-skating. I know that she loved going to the ice rink in Altrincham, and that was one of her favourite pastimes when she was younger. When I asked her about religion, she always said she was a heathen (this fairly a-religious parental combination may well have had some bearing the fact that I was never christened). She had a hard life growing up in Rhodes, near Middleton, because her Father, Fred Howard, died when she was quite young, and when she was a teenager, she had to take over as head of the household when my Nana was unwell and look after her younger sister Maureen. Once, when my Nana became ill, she was in hospital in Oldham, and my Mother walked from Rhodes and back to visit her because she didn't have the bus fare. She was caring and a great cook and knitter (of which more later).

My Mother's mother, Nana Thomas (formerly Howard) – it was never Grandma, people have Mas and Nanas in my part of the world – lived in a council house on Kelvin Avenue in Rhodes, with my Grandad Ernie. Ernie was a great bloke who looked a bit like Alf Garnett, as did lots of blokes in those days, but without the moustache. He had small round glasses and always wore braces. He was a real stout ale[9] and flat cap man. At that time, I didn't realise he wasn't my real Grandad – who had died just after the Second World War. Annie and Ernie Thomas were great fun, both working class people who'd had fairly hard lives through the wars and a depression but hadn't been ground down by the experience. Sadly, Ernie died when I was about six and my Nana never remarried. My Nana was as tough as old boots and full of life and lived to the grand old age of 95. She had retired when I was a child. She visited the local old folks club to play whist and have a cuppa, and liked a glass of beer. She also liked a flutter on the horses. Her bets were small, but she was good at picking winners.

My paternal grandparents were Grandad James and Nana Ethel Thorp, who lived at 49, Park Road, Sale. With them lived my Dad's older brother Uncle Clifford (whose real name was George – but he preferred to be called Clifford). My parents also lived here for a short time after

---

[9] Stout seems to have almost disappeared nowadays. Guinness is still served in most pubs but bottled stouts and brown ales were very popular at the time. Now making a come back as craft beer.

they married, and I can still remember the house clearly. It was a large red brick Victorian semi and remained almost exactly the same, frozen in time until Uncle George "Clifford" Thorp died in April 1995.

George 'Clifford' Thorp

My Dad had another older brother Uncle Jim, who lived with Auntie Irene in Old Trafford. Jim was 13 years older than my Dad, and he was the caretaker of Trafford Technical College. Their house was attached to the college. They had two children, Cheryl and Simon, and later, Helen. Jim fought in the Second World War in the Navy as a sailor on the Baltic convoys and was posthumously awarded a medal. He had a hard war and never used to talk about it.

Uncle Jim (or Slim as he was known to his shipmates) enlisted in the Fleet Air Arm in 1941 when he was just 19 After stints at various training bases around the UK and on other ships, he became a crew member on board the escort aircraft carrier HMS Vindex and almost immediately embarked on his first perilous journey to Russia in one of the now celebrated and commemorated Arctic Russian Convoys. The convoys were devised by Churchill and advisers to supply the Russians with munitions including tanks and planes, artillery, as well as food and medical supplies to enable them to maintain an effective Eastern front which would in turn allow Britain and its allies to focus on attacking German-occupied Europe from the West.

Convoys normally comprised a good number of merchant ships escorted by one or two aircraft carriers carrying submarine hunting Swordfish as well as Sea Hurricanes and Grumman Hellcats to tackle attacks by German fighter and bomber aircraft. The escort would also include other vessels such as destroyers and cruisers, mine-sweepers, and anti-submarine trawlers.

Jim survived 2 years of extreme danger and dreadful conditions. Once the German threat in Europe was at an end, the ship, with Jim still manfully doing his job and now promoted to leading seaman, was dispatched to the Pacific to assist US colleagues in their fight against the Japanese. At one point, the Vindex was moored in Australia and Jim joked that some of his most dangerous times in WWII came during episodes of shore leave in some of the more exciting bars that country was able to offer up to visiting sailors.

En route to the East, the Vindex was moored in Valetta Harbour in Malta, which was still under threat from Axis air and seaborne attack. Jim had an aerial photograph (now sadly lost) of a clear Mediterranean sea and three German U-boats lurking outside the submarine nets drawn across the entrance to the harbour awaiting the embarkation of the British naval vessels on their way to the Pacific[10].

Many years later, at one of Jim and Irene's parties, I asked him what had been the most exciting thing that happened in the war. He told me that he had been drinking on leave in a bar in Glasgow and someone had bet him he couldn't sit on a pint pot on the bar – he did but fell off and broke his leg! Jim had a great, dry sense of humour and was always ready to crack a few one-liners.

Auntie Rene was one of the warmest and funniest persons I have ever met. She had time for everyone and was always laughing and full of hilarious stories, which had us in stitches and could keep people entertained for hours.[11] That was a generation whose early lives had been dominated by the war and who had learned to be very tough and stoical. Many had suffered hardships that we can't imagine now, but they were tough and made the best of life.

---

[10] Thanks to cousin Simon for this information.
[11] Sadly Jim and Rene have now passed on but are warmly remembered by all who knew them.

In the Beginning

Left to right: James Thorp, Ethel Thorp, Mavis Thorp, Geoffrey Thorp and Annie Howard at my mother and fathers' wedding

Cheryl   Simon

Cheryl and Simon were a few years older than me, and Helen much younger. I enjoyed meeting up with them at holiday time. Our families went to North Wales and stayed in caravans near the beach. This was quite common for families from Manchester and the North West at the time.

Mum's sister, Auntie Maureen, had married Brian Dickens, and we used to visit his mother's house on Carrington Lane. For some reason, we all always called Brian's mother Mrs. Dickens. I remember her clearly with her silvery white hair.

James and Irene Thorp (nee Bithell) on honeymoon in the Isle of Man 1950

Brian and Maureen emigrated, in the early 1960s, to South Africa and later moved on to Australia. We never visited them in South Africa, but my Nana made several journeys to see them. In fact, in her old age, she became quite a globetrotter visiting both countries and finally settling in Sydney in 1987.

In the Beginning

My Mum's family was working class, and my Dad's family was lower middle class. They were close enough, in those days, to have mixed and worked with, and understood working class people. Grandad James Thorp had been a salesman for most of his working life and had done well. He had bought his rented house at No. 49 Park Road in Sale in 1959 and had a black Ford Popular. As a result, I was brought up with a mixture of values and ideas from both classes. This had its advantages because it meant I was always able to mix with working class people and fit in. However, even my time later on at grammar school never fully prepared me for mixing with the real middle classes in later life.

One of the saddest things about my early years was the fact that three out of my four grandparents had died by the mid 60s. My maternal Grandfather Fred died in 1941.

Very early days on Blackpool beach

My second hand memories of him from my Nana Thomas are not very clear, but I recall that she told me that he drowned in a flood in Middleton. Up to the time of writing, I have been unable to verify this. He had a bother called Sam Howard. My Nanna told me Fred had invented a dye, and I think he and Sam worked in the chemical industry, probably for ICI. I have since found out that Fred died at the

Me and my Nana in Southport

age of 43, probably of tuberculosis. His occupation was textile dying, printing, and heavy printing machine process worker.

I can hardly remember my paternal Grandfather and Grandmother – though I can recall my Dad telling me that my Grandmother, who was a devout catholic, believed it was against God's will for man to land on the moon and therefore it would never happen. What would she have thought if she had lived to see it?

Chapter 2
AND IN THE PAST

Before I move on, it's time for a bit more family history. I have many photographs that my father took but, alas, not much in the way of documents. However, when my Uncle Clifford died, I visited 49, Park Road, Sale and found a treasure trove of old documents and

Great Grandfather James Thorp, Great Grandmother Mary-Ann, with Lillian and James. Taken early 1900s

photographs. Using this, I was able to put together a Thorp family tree and discover who my Great Grandfather and Grandmother were. The documents show that my Grandfather James Thorp was born in 1897 and died in 1963. My Great Grandparents Mary Ann and James Thorp Lived at 67 Rowsley Street, Beswick, Manchester. James Thorp was a tailor.

During WWI, James Thorp (junior) was in the 7th Manchesters regiment. He was based in Cairo and was wounded and treated in Malta. He also fell sick and ended up in hospital in Alexandria. At that time, he had a girlfriend called Emily Houssely. There are letters which show correspondence between Emily and James's parents who she addresses and Dear Mother and Dear Father. The relationship came to a tragic end. We (the family) don't know

Postcard from Emily to James based in Cairo

why but we think Emily was French, and it was because his parents didn't approve of him having a foreign girlfriend. There is a heartfelt letter from James to Emily apologising for breaking up with her. James went on to marry Ethel Sorby, who we know also lived in Beswick. There are also some documents from his time n the army concerning his injures and payments, including a payment of £1.14 shillings sent to his mother in Beswick.

Emily's postcard message to James

I did find a photo of James and Ethel Thorp with their children James, and George (Clifford) (see below). My father wasn't born when the photo was taken. I know that James and Ethel Thorp were bon viveurs and enjoyed partying. James was always smartly dressed, cigarette in hand, and was a bit of a lad.

Alas, I haven't been able to find any family documents from my mother's side of the family, but there are some photos I can share. I have a photo of My Nana's wedding to Ernie Thomas and some photos of me on holiday with them wher I was a kid.

James and Ethel Thorp with their sons James and George 'Clifford'

And in the Past

Ernie and Annie's wedding L-R Brian Dickens, Maureen Dickens, Ernie, Annie, Dad, Mum, Unknown - I expect that this is Ernie's son

FAMILY TREE

This is my family tree going back to Great Grandfather and Grandmother on my Father's side. I still have more work to do to identify my Great Grandparents on my Mother's side of the family.

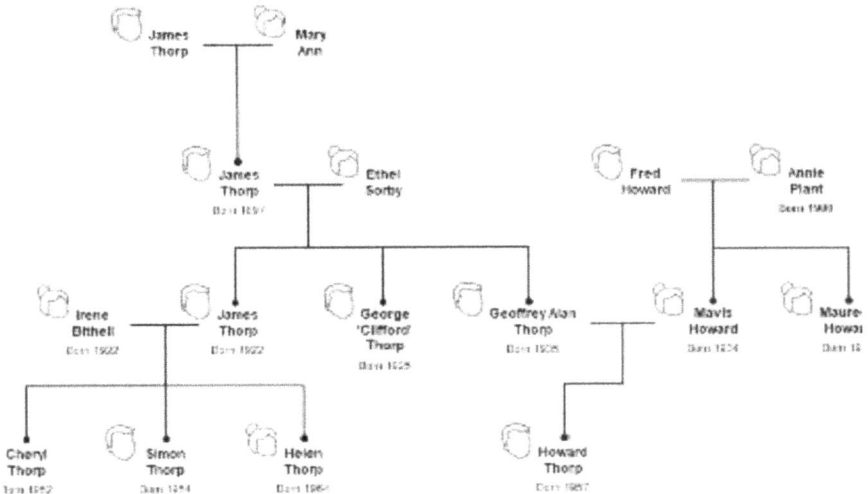

Chapter 3
EARLY DAYS

Apart from the trains near our house and playing with friends, one of the earliest things I can remember about growing up in Sale was a local shop that used to sell carpets and had a box out the front with small free sample tiles in it. I had an obsession with collecting all the different types and colours and used to take one every time I passed the shop with my Mum. Eventually, she made me a rug out of all the pieces which I thought was great!

I guess I must have been about 3 years old when we moved to a brand new estate of semi-detached houses in Alkrington near Middleton, in north Manchester. We lived at no. 86 Warwick Road. Middleton was an independent Borough at the time and became part of Rochdale MBC in the local government re-organisation in 1974.

It was quite a thing at the time that my parents had decided to buy their own home. Many people lived in rented accommodation or council housing, and lower middle class people were just starting to get on the housing ladder. This undoubtedly involved sacrifices since we were hard up until I was in my early teens. The move was pretty momentous stuff for me. I was really excited to try and help with the unloading of the removal van – especially my precious carpet. When we moved in to our new home, the houses at the end of Warwick Road weren't finished and they made a great playground. There were piles of sand and bricks around and, most importantly, new friends.

There was a gang of us on our bit of Warwick Road which I remained a part of for most of the next decade. There were sisters Beverly and Alison, and Julie, Alan, and baby brother Kevin and the brothers Chris and Terry. Chris was the oldest, then Julie and I, who were about the same age, then, Beverly, then Alan, and Terry and Alison were a couple of years younger[12]. Those things are very

---

[12] We didn't all go to the same local primary school. Lancashire has historically had a high proportion of Catholics. I went to the local C of E primary school as did Beverly and Alison.

important when you are young where even being a year older can make a great difference.

Chris tended to be a bit of a loner and not involved with the rest of us as much. I think it had a lot to do with the fact that he had a gammy arm which was caused by polio. He used to wear a plastic brace as a support on his arm. Some kind of handicap due to Polio was much more common in those days (my Dad also had a weakened leg due to polio)[13]. Kids can be pretty cruel and I guess Chris got a lot of stick for having Polio, but he certainly knew how to look after himself.

The Thorp Family at Warwick Road – note Fred the tortoise who met an unfortunate end

I guess that I was the leader of the gang being the oldest male (ok this was the 60s) – though Julie was definitely the bossiest. When I was about eight, she split my head open with a coal shovel[14] because

---

[13] There was a polio epidemic in Britain in the 1950s and the disease was much commoner before the introduction of the Salk vaccine.
[14] Another reminder of the times. Although the houses were new semis in 1960 they still had coal fires.

I had spent the afternoon playing in a tent with Beverly and Alison in their back garden! Hell had no fury….! This wasn't the only hazard in playing with Beverly and Alison – they had a very intimidating mother who didn't really approve of her daughters playing with urchins like me and Terry! Her favourite saying was "Girls should play with girls and boys should play with boys!" – any excuse to keep the boys away from her precious daughters.

The Gang: Left to right: Me, Terry, Alison and Beverly

Chris and Terry were part of one of the more interesting families in a fairly dull but cosy suburban street. It was a catholic[15] working class

---

[15] Why do I keep mentioning religion – because it meant something at the time. Not that any of us were religious of course but there was religious segregation in terms of schools – something the religionists in the current Labour government are desperate to revive (written in a time of New Labour).

family which appeared to live completely chaotically. I never saw their mother and father very often. Chris and Terry had several brothers and sisters, some older and at least one younger. Who knows how many or what their names were, but there seemed to be a lot of them living in the house at any one time. Terry and Chris, like many kids in those days, used to live on a staple diet of chips – proper chips made from sliced potatoes and cooked in lard in a chip pan – or chip butties on white bread.

Terry made some chips for me one lunchtime when he must have been only about eight years old. It was one of the first survival skills he'd learned. Of course the neighbours, all of whom were moving up, probably weren't too amused to find this family in their midst. Many had moved from council houses and back-to-back terraces, to escape to their suburban Shangri-La.

On my eighth birthday, my Dad had bought me a swing which was quite a present then. I had a brilliant birthday party with jelly, fairy cakes, crisps, and lots of other good stuff made by my Mum. When Terry turned up and my Dad asked him what he wanted, he replied "chips"! He then proceeded to take a bite out of a glass that contained lemonade and later on managed to break the swing by snapping one of the ropes!

We used to do some pretty dangerous and daft things when we were fighting, particularly throwing stones. There was real danger if you were a good shot like I was, and too young and daft to think of the potential consequences. I remember once hitting someone just above the eye with a stone, and knocking out another lad's tooth with a casually flicked stone – not an easy one to explain when his parents came round to our house!

We used to play lots of games, camp out in our gardens, and play with lots of toys. Toy guns were all the rage, and we used to have cap guns which banged when you fired them. Cowboy films were very popular in those days, and we used to play cowboys and Indians. We had roller skates and made buggies out of old prams. My favourite possession was my bicycle, and I used to spend hours cycling round the surrounding area. We were rarely inside even in the Winter, partly because most of the new house owners were house proud and didn't want kids in their house.

One summer in 1966, three police officers were shot and killed while on duty in Shepherds Bush, London[16]. The event shocked the whole nation, and our gang decided to raise some money for the policemen's families by holding a 'Batman Fair'. Batman was on the telly and all the rage with us at the time, and we made a Batmobile, dressed up and managed to extract money from locals and unsuspecting passers by which was passed on to the families.

Although we lived in Alkrington, it was very much a suburb of Middleton, and one of the posher bits. Middleton was my home town. In the 1960s, Middleton was an independent borough with its own council and Town Hall. The centre of Middleton was an attractive place with two sets of central gardens and a bus station. If you can imagine a figure of eight on a north–south axis with the gardens inside the loops of the eight, that is roughly what the town centre was like. The gardens were attractive and well looked after, with floral displays. They were surrounded by shops, banks, and pubs.

Nikolaus Pevsner says[17] – "Middleton has not the gloom of so many South Lancashire towns of its size". I agree with him. Middleton, in those days, had lovely central gardens, some buildings with real character, its very own UCP tripe shop in the centre of town, and the legendary chippy Thompsons, better known as 'Tommy's!

Here is a description of Alkrington in 1873:

Alkrington is a township, in the parish of Prestwich, hundred of Salford, union and county court district of Oldham, purely agricultural,

---

[16] On the afternoon of Friday 12th August 1966, DS Head, PC Fox and DC Wombwell were driving their Triumph 2000 Q car, Foxtrot Eleven, around F Division, which included the areas of East Acton, Hammersmith, Shepherd's Bush and Fulham. At about 3 in the afternoon they spotted an old battered blue Vauxhall estate driving around East Acton. The car was being driven by its owner John Edward Witney. Witney, a 36-year-old unemployed man was well known to the police and had a long record with ten previous convictions for petty theft. His passengers were 37-year-old Scot John Duddy and 30-year-old Harry Maurice Roberts. As they examined the suspect vehicle DC Wombwell was shot by Harry Roberts. DS head fled only to be shot in the back by Duddy who also killed PC Fox who had remained in the police car.

[17] In his book South Lancashire.

5 miles north from Manchester and about half-a-mile from Middleton. It forms part of the ecclesiastical district of Tonge-cum-Alkrington. Alkrington hall, the seat of Mrs. Lees, is a noble brick building, situated of an eminence, and is surrounded by a well wooded park of 80 acres; it commands a fine view of the surrounding country. Mrs. Lees is lady of the manor. The principal landowners are Mrs. Lees & John & Joseph Lees. The area is 798 acres; gross estimated rental, £2,158; rateable value, £1,710; the population in 1871 was 388; the population of the ecclesiastical district is 5,503[18].

The lady of the manor had long gone when I first visited Alkrington Hall, which had been turned into flats. I spent many happy hours playing there and in Alkrington woods, part of the grounds.

The town and borough of Middleton has an interesting history. It was very much a Lancashire mill town being the home of Samuel Bamford, the radical and writer. In August 1819, Bamford led a group from Middleton to St Peter's Fields, to attend a meeting pressing for parliamentary reform and the repeal of the Corn Laws, where they witnessed the Peterloo Massacre. Bamford was arrested and charged with treason. He ended up serving a year in gaol.

Alongside the mills, such as Warwick Mill near the town centre, there is the Old Boar's Head – an Elizabethan timber-framed pub. The pub still contains the sessions room where the magistrates used to hear cases. There is an old Grammar School and an interesting and unusual prominently sited church, St Leonards, with a wooden tower from c.1667[19].

The "Flodden Window", in the church's sanctuary, is thought to be the oldest war memorial in the United Kingdom. It memorialises on it the names of the archers of Middleton who fought at the Battle of Flodden Field (1513), the largest battle ever fought between the kingdoms of Scotland and England.

---

[18] Post Office Directory of Lancashire Excluding Manchester 1873.
[19] Nicklaus Pevsner - The buildings of England - South Lancashire.

Middleton then had its own independent brewery in J W Lees, and a railway station at Middleton Junction. Then, of course, there are the legendary Moonrakers of Middleton. Moonraker refers to the legend of poachers who, upon seeing the local constabulary, would throw their catch into a pond and begin raking the reflection of the moon on the water, giving the excuse that they were trying to recover the 'green cheese'.

St Leonards Church, Middleton 1960s

Things went badly for Middleton in the 1970s. In 1974, there was a local government reorganisation that created the metropolitan counties, including Greater Manchester. So we were moved out of Lancashire into a new county, and Middleton was subsumed into the metropolitan borough of Rochdale.

Middleton lost its independence, and at the same time, a new Arndale Centre and bus station was built in the south part of the town centre destroying part of the gardens. The shiny new shopping centre seemed like progress, but it had really ripped the heart out of the town. For me, Middleton became a shadow of its former self. There is a new centre for concerts but is a building of no great merit. The place has the look and feel of a traffic island. At least Long Street – the site of the Old Boar's and St Leonards – has kept most of its charm, though it still looks neglected.[20]

The Old Boars Head, Middleton 1960s

---

[20] To be fair I haven't visited Middleton for many years. No doubt it has improved since I last saw it?

Chapter 4
FAMILY LIFE

Not having brothers and sisters meant that I was mostly the centre of attention as far as my parents were concerned. However, they were determined not to spoil me, which meant that I didn't get my own way like some children (with brothers and sisters) do. I was lucky that we lived in a semi-detached house from a fairly early age so that I was able to have a room of my own and a garden to play in.

Many of the kids that I knew had to share a room with a brother or sister. When I was very small, I was afraid of the dark, so I used to have a small lamp in my bedroom – which probably made things worse by casting shadows. We also had a central heating system which used to make strange noises. So much for a new house! – the timbers used to creak at night like a haunted mansion!

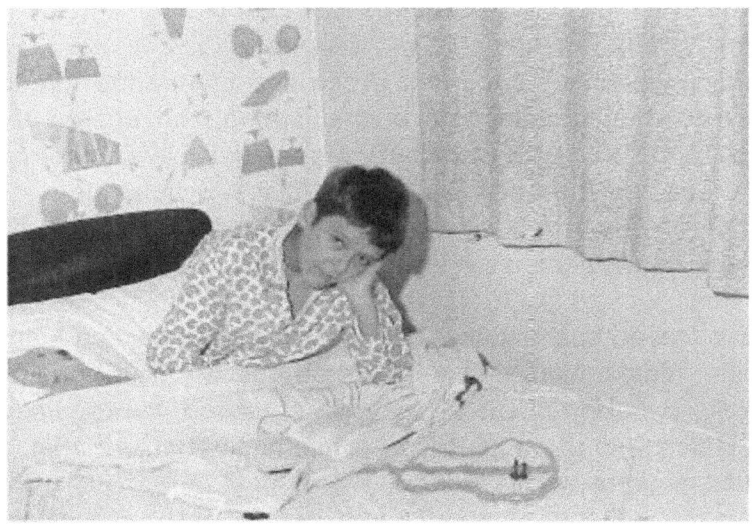

Reading in bed. My bedroom at Warwick Road – note teddy – alas long since lost, my groovy guitar counterpane, and pyjamas

Over the years, my bedroom was the scene of mighty battles with my large collection of Airfix soldiers. I even had an excellent

Airfix castle which was frequently under attack. Among the epic re-enactments were the American civil war, Waterloo, and Robin Hood and his merry men versus bad King John. I used to spend hours on these battles. As I got older, they became more and more sophisticated.

I also spent many happy hours playing with my railway set, Hornby double O. I had a Stevenson's rocket which was so fast it would never take the corners! It even had a small bottle of oil with a dropper, so that you could drop oil into the funnel and produce smoke. Given that it had an electrified track that you could get shocks off, would any of that be allowed now? Many other toys shared that space, including my faithful Teddy bear, various action men, Daleks, toy robots, Zeroids – which were robot like creatures – and the unsurpassable Johnny Seven OMA (One Man Army) – just about the most powerful plastic weapon ever invented – it fired plastic bullets and rockets and even had a grenade launcher.

I also had loads of toy cars from Morris Minors to James Bond's Aston Martin – complete with ejector seat – and trucks, tractors, and fire engines. One of my besties was a box set of Chipperfield's Circus vehicles I got for Xmas.

Comics were very important to me and my friends. We looked forward to them coming out and swapped and shared them. I used to read TV21 with Dan Dare, Marvel comics, and comics like Wham! and the Beano. I really liked Classics Illustrated – comic books of famous novels, like Ivanhoe[21]. My parents used to buy me Look and Learn because it was considered to be educational and improving.

I also played board games with my parents, including Monopoly, Scrabble, Mastermind, chess, and draughts. My Dad bought me a wonderful travelling chess set which I treasured. He regularly beat me at chess, and when I finally beat him aged about 12, that, ahem, was the last game we played.

From my bedroom window, I had a view out onto the back gardens of Warwick Road and Cheltenham Road. In the distance, I could see the mill chimneys of Middleton and Bury and the pale green line of the Pennine hills around Rossendale.

---

[21] I still have my copy.

I always enjoyed a brew, a cup of builder's tea, and the milk was delivered each morning by the milkman in his electric milk float. The milk was in glass bottles. In the winter, it sometimes froze and local birds had the cheeky habit of pecking a hole in the foil cap and having a drink. In the summer, when it was hot, I'd be quite happy to have a drink of corporation pop, as tap water was known in those days.

One of the best things about my childhood was food! My Mum was a housewife, which meant she didn't go out to work. It was not that unusual in the 60s for even working class mothers to stay at home to look after children; many had part-time, rather than full-time jobs. It was still assumed that husbands should "bring home the bacon" – or should it be spam? Spam, a brand of cooked pork which came in tins, was still popular in those days, and Monty Python wrote a famous song about it. Spam has a very different meaning these days.

Being at home gave my Mum time to cook and she was very, very good at it, and she made great brews. She also made bread, fabulous pastry and cakes, and the best meat and potato pies I've ever had. Sunday lunches definitely need a mention. We used to have ours late on Sunday afternoon. Roast chicken, lamb, and occasionally beef made it the meal of the week, usually with a rare luxury like a glass of beer for my Dad. Vegetables and fruit were seasonal then. You could only get leeks and sprouts in the autumn and winter. Mum was also fairly adventurous at a time when most families in Britain ate "meat and two veg" at meal times. She used to cook things like curries, spaghetti bolognese, and beef stroganoff.

This was reasonably adventurous for the early 60s, though curries tended to be made with 'curry powder' rather than separate spices and chillies or garlic, and contained things like sultanas. It meant that we very rarely had pre-cooked or tinned food, except for Batchelors soup and baked beans, and take-aways weren't nearly as common or popular then. When I asked my Mum what we were having for tea, she usually said, "Two jumps a' cupboard and a bite a' knob!".

This was the age of 'manufactured' food like Smash – instant potato mash and Angel Delight – a powder that was mixed with milk to make a sweet moose-like dessert. Science had intervened, and processed food was thought to be better for you than natural stuff – after all, it had added vitamins! This was very much how food was sold to people in the 60s and 70s before scares about food additives began to turn people back to natural food.

The only take-out meal we regularly ate was fish and chips – which came wrapped in newspaper to keep it warm, but things were beginning to change. Still, I must have been 14 when I had my first Chinese and Indian take-aways. In Manchester, Chinese restaurants came earlier than Indian. There was already a Chinese community established in Manchester before most of the first curry houses opened.

As for the fish and chips, we used to have this on Friday nights as a treat when Nana Thomas, who lived in a council flat in Rhodes, came round to join us after being collected by my Dad. Thompsons – Tommys – in Middleton used to do the best fish, chips, and mushy peas on the planet!

When Nana Thomas came and joined us on Fridays, it was a treat for me because she always used to give me a shilling and bring me some chocolate, usually a Mars bar, which was my favourite[22]. Despite not being in any way religious, we always used to have fish on Fridays. A Catholic habit but one followed by many irreligious families like ours.

There were no MacDonalds, Burger Kings, Starbucks, or fancy sandwich bars, but there was the aforementioned UCP tripe shop and the odd 'caff' or greasy spoon. Middleton used to have one with a claim to fame – a café called 'The Full Monty' – well before the film was made. Since the film with the same name, there have been many suggestions about where this expression originated. My favourite explanation is that it probably originated with Field Marshall Montgomery's (Monty's) liking for a hearty breakfast, with the English breakfast being a particular favourite in greasy spoons and transport cafes.

Tastes in wine amongst the working and lower middle classes were generally not very sophisticated (I can't speak for the upper orders!). Wine was for special occasions only, such as birthdays, Christmas, courting, and impressing visitors, and French red – Piat d'Or – and German white – Liebfraumilch and Blue Nun – were about all you could hope for. Our family never had wine with a meal at home except

---

[22] Up until Nana left for Australia after my 30th Birthday I still got multi-packs of Mars Bars every Christmas. They were always appreciated.

at Christmas dinner and the odd Sunday lunch when I was older. Dad sometimes had beer with a meal, and Mum preferred cider.

Having said that, beer for mass consumption wasn't any better than the wine that was on offer. This was the age of Watneys, who made gassy, tasteless beers, and Party Sevens. The latter contained seven pints of pretty grim beer. It was very popular at parties though. Beer and soft drinks like Coca Cola came in glass bottles on which you could get a deposit back before the new-fangled craze for cans took over. But you had to have a can opener even to get beer out of a can; there were no ring pulls; you punched holes on opposite sides of the top of the can with a beer can opener and poured into a glass.

Nearly all home meals we had were eaten at the dining room table, and the usual routine was me coming in from school, watching a bit of telly before Dad got home at about five o'clock[23] and then sitting down to eat shortly after. And yes, Dad did used to come home, put on his slippers, sit in an armchair, and read a bit of the paper, before tea was ready. He even used to smoke a pipe at one time! That sounds Chomondley-Warnerish by 21st century standards, but it was by no means unusual then. Very few people had freezers of any size, and TV dinners were things that existed only in the future and, like most things we were about to experience, in the USA. Eating food as a family was an important daily ritual, and I was expected to observe various rules like eating all my food and having to ask to leave the table.

Christmases were very special! Usually, I was awake by about 6 am on Christmas morning because I was too excited to sleep. My parents were pretty crafty about hiding presents and always managed to sneak them into my room after I actually had gone to sleep. Early in the morning, there was the ritual of opening the presents. We always had my Nana over later on Christmas Day. Before we collected her, Dad and I would go round to see Uncle Jim and Auntie Irene in Old Trafford and then on to 49 Park Road in Sale to visit Uncle Clifford, who was a virtual recluse, while Mum got Christmas dinner ready. We always used to take Clifford a cooked chicken and some mince pies made by Mum.

---

[23] His hours were 8.30 – 4.30 rather than 9 – 5.

I was quite scared when I was young visiting Uncle Clifford because he was over six foot tall and fairly intimidating – with his squarish head and cropped hair, he used to loom over me and looked a bit like Frankenstein to me. He was very miserly and only had forty watt light bulbs in the gloomy house. When you switched on a light, the room seemed to get darker. On a bleak winter's evening, visiting Clifford could be very spooky stuff. We used to arrive as it was going dark and go round to the back door (Clifford never used the front door). Dad would bang on the door and shout for "George". After a few minutes silence, we'd hear the sound of half a dozen or more bolts being drawn back, and chains being removed, before the door was unlocked and opened. We were then ushered into the drab small back parlour and kitchen by Clifford, who was always wearing a threadbare dressing gown. He used to hibernate in the winter to save money. You could smell the gloom.

The house was freezing cold inside, and the first thing Dad did was to go into the back parlour and put the gas fire on. Uncle Clifford would then show us some of the latest bargains he'd bought, such as bags of sugar or tins of Vim, and tell us all about his ailments and visits to the doctor. What they were, I can't recall now, but he always seemed to have at least half a dozen illnesses on the go. The small dining table in the back parlour was covered with his medicines. With the number of pills he took, if he been any smaller, he'd have rattled. It felt like a black and white film of a Dickens novel, almost like being John Mills in Miss Havisham's house in the classic film of Great Expectations directed by David Lean (1946).

He always talked at us in a very loud voice, as if we were deaf, while I sat on the freezing sofa looking on in amazement, wondering what he was going to do next, hardly daring to speak, and glad that my Dad was there. Fortunately, it was obvious he respected my Dad and always deferred to him. He was pleased to see me and always used to give me some small present. Then, at some stage in the proceedings, he'd have a rant about the 'neighbours' and various locals who he thought were plotting against him. He'd also proudly show us some improvement he'd made to the house – which usually involved fitting yet another lock to the back door. He seemed to regard himself as the caretaker rather than the tenant and probably felt some guilt about living in the house which also belonged to my Dad and Uncle Jim.

Had there been a nuclear war at any time in the past 40 years, Uncle Clifford would have been one of the best prepared people in the country and probably one of the few survivors. He had a huge cupboard stuffed with tins of food, packets of washing powder, and even things like bleach. You could have stocked a small pharmacist with his medicines. He also had a ritual to show us how well prepared for burglars he was by brandishing a large carving knife and giving a native Indian war whoop – thank God no one ever tried to burgle the house! After the usual admonishments from my Dad to spend more money on light bulbs and heating and stop fooling around with knives, we headed homewards to light and warmth and sanity, via my Nana's.

Visits to Uncle Clifford's became less frightening as I got older, but they were always sad and eerie and made a big impression on me. Clifford was a great eccentric, a genuine family skeleton in the cupboard, and I was moved by my Dad's obvious concern and compassion for him. It would have been so easy to have fobbed Clifford off onto the social services. As it was, he led a strange but independent life which gave him dignity and self respect. Odd as he was, he was largely treated tolerantly by the local people in Sale. I'll never forget my Dad telling me about the harrowing experience he had visiting Clifford in a mental hospital and how he wouldn't have wished that on anybody.

When Uncle Clifford died in 1995, he had saved over £40,000 out of his invalidity benefits over the years due to his Spartan existence. My Dad, who sorted out Uncle Clifford's affairs and arranged the funeral with help from my cousin Simon, was amazed to discover that the hermit of Park Road was quite well known locally. He used to visit many of the local shops and chat to the owners and customers. When he popped into the local bank, he was sometimes given a cup of tea by the staff. Despite his eccentricity, many people remembered him and had a kind word to say about him.

After the visit to Uncle Clifford's and collecting Nana on the way home, there followed the time-honoured routine of too much good food and drink and telly back in Warwick Road. I loved the Christmas Tree, decorations, crackers, and all the trimmings. The Christmas meal was always a time when my Mum excelled herself with a turkey, stuffing, sausages, roast potatoes, sprouts, carrots, lovely gravy, home-made Xmas pud, and those wonderful mince pies. In the evening, we were treated to shows like Eric Morecambe and Ernie Wise at their very best. Along with the rest of the, overindulged, country, we sat back and laughed.

On Boxing day evening, we would usually go over to Uncle Jim's and Auntie Irene's for their legendary Xmas party. The house was full and the beer flowed – the joint was always jumping. Jim and Irene certainly knew how to party, and from an early age, I thoroughly enjoyed being with them, their family, and friends. The house was full of laughter, and my Auntie Rene and Uncle Jim's warmth and humour lit up what was a fairly gloomy corner of Manchester.

This is me at the Clayton Aniline Xmas party

My Dad also used to take me every year to the kids Christmas party that was held at his workplace, with plenty of cakes, ice cream, jelly, and entertainers. It was great!

Apart from her cooking, my Mum also used to knit a lot. This is something that seems almost to have disappeared nowadays. She used to sit in her armchair and knit regularly whilst watching the telly. She produced lots of really good stuff, mainly jumpers, things like

Aran sweaters,[24] and baby clothes. It was a very practical thing to do and saved money. One of her other favourite pastimes was doing cryptic crosswords. She used to do the Manchester Guardian[25] crossword every day.

Beloved Tinky

My Dad's big hobby when not working was photography; he had several single lens reflex cameras and set up a darkroom in our 'box room'. He earned extra money in his own time by doing weddings. When I was a little older, I used to go and help him. Dad also spent a fair amount of his time gardening in our small back garden and

---

[24] To my eternal regret I no longer have any of the jumpers. I used to have half a dozen and they were all very good.
[25] Now The Guardian.

used to produce cabbages, potatoes, carrots, and spring onions from his vegetable patch. He also used to keep Carp in a big tank in the back garden, and later the garden pond. Speaking of the pond, our beloved tortoise Fred came to a sad end when he fell in the pond and drowned. We also had a cat called Tinky for many years. I loved him and was gutted when he died.

The big payoff came in the early 70s when Dad entered a photographic competition and won a colour television worth £250 – a substantial sum for the time. Up until then, we had had a tired old collection of black and white televisions, and initially no outdoor TV aerial. This meant using an indoor aerial which had to be moved to a different position every time you changed channel. It also meant that the picture was very unreliable and varied with things like the weather – which made it look like it was snowing on the picture. Sometimes, you had to fiddle about with the aerial for ages to get a decent picture. Of course, there were no remote controls, so you had to get up to change channels – good job there were only three choices! Many people used to rent TVs in those days, but we had our own.

One of the black and white tellies had a spectacular ending. One summer's evening whilst watching, Mum and I noticed smoke coming from out of the back of the telly. Mum rushed to the lounge door and shouted upstairs "Geoff, the television's on fire!". I could hear muffled curses as Dad, who was in the bog, broke off what he was doing, and came hurtling downstairs, still clutching his trousers. I watched awestruck as he grabbed the telly, raced through to the kitchen, and managed to hurl it through the (open) back door into the garden (what he would have done if it was winter I don't know). Anyway, the colour TV was a great hit and a major prize too.

One embarrassing incident I need to mention was the scouts. When I was about 12, I decided to join the local scouts group. I timed it badly because I'd only attended a couple of sessions before it was 'Bob a Job' week. This was when the scouts used to volunteer to help people with tasks, like washing a car, in return for sixpence which went towards scout funding. I couldn't be bothered to do any tasks, so I retired in shame not wanting them to know I hadn't collected anything. Nowadays, that kind of thing would probably be regarded as unsafe since it involved you boys going into the houses of strangers.

Family Life

I was lucky not to have any serious illnesses as a kid, though I did have four perfectly good teeth removed when I was about seven because I had a small mouth with jumbled teeth. I had gas, and I was a grim experience. Of course, I then had to wear a brace which was embarrassing. In those days, the universal cures for most childhood bouts of flu and colds were aspirin, Vics Vapour Rub, which I liked, Olbas Oil, and Lucozade!

At Lyme Park with my Mum, Dad & Nana - 1965

My parents used to like getting out into the country, for either a drive or a walk. Dad used to take us out on Sundays, and we'd visit old country houses like Chatsworth in Derbyshire, Hall I' th' Wood in Bolton, and Little Moreton Hall in Cheshire. We must have visited most of the stately homes, abbeys, gardens, and castles of northern England, north Wales, and north Midlands during my childhood. Going for a drive on a Sunday afternoon then was very much the done thing. Families used to take their flasks of coffee, sandwiches, and head for the great outdoors. Of course, to get out and pose, you had to have a car, and we got one when I was about six. Up 'til then, my Dad had gone to work on his Honda 90.

Unfortunately for me, the car was a Reliant Robin! – a type of three-wheeler which is now, fortunately, extinct. This was a mega-embarrassment for me since all my friends took the mickey unmercifully. Their dads had proper cars with four wheels! I cringed when we turned up at school for parents evening in the Reliant. Nonetheless, the 'Noddy Car' managed to get us all over the country and provided sterling service despite the fact that the top speed was about 50 miles per hour (downhill with a following wind).

Holidays always took place in Britain. I didn't go abroad until I was 19. That probably wasn't untypical while I was a child, although by the time I was a teenager, more and more people were going further afield to Europe, especially Spain. In the early days, we didn't have a car, so it was the bus for us. We had to go by bus from Alkrington to Chorlton Street bus station in Manchester. From there, you could catch a coach to anywhere in the country. We rarely travelled by rail, which was more expensive, but I can remember travelling with my Mum and Nana to Southport on the steam train from Middleton Junction station. We also had days out at the seaside, usually Southport, but sometimes Blackpool. My Nana preferred Southport because it was posher than Blackpool. Whenever we went, I loved to play with my bucket and spade, building sandcastles on the beach.

For several years up to about the age of 9 or 10, we used to catch a North Western Coach to Penmeanmawr, near Conwy (Conway in those days), and stayed in a caravan in Dwygfylchi. Sometimes, we went with Jim and Irene and my cousins Cheryl and Simon. I can remember pebbly beaches, having to cross the railway line to get to the beach and swimming in the sea.

When we visited places like Conwy, and I used to catch crabs with a line and bait in the harbour. The Welsh castles such as Beaumaris, Conwy, and Caernarfon were fantastic for a Robin Hood fan like me, and I can remember charging up to the battlements brandishing my plastic sword. Other places we visited frequently on holidays were the Lake District and Yorkshire Dales.

When I was 10, I went youth hosteling to Grasmere for a few days with Dad travelling there by coach from Manchester. We had good weather and climbed Steel Fell and Helm Crag. I really enjoyed the trip – apart from my Dad's snoring which kept me awake. Coming home on the Sunday, we missed the coach in Grasmere village (in reality, it never turned up) and were stuck. Fortunately, I had enough money, just thirty bob[26], which I had saved from pocket money, to pay for another night in the youth hostel because my father was broke – there were no cash machines or credit cards; if banks were shut, you couldn't get money.

If you were lucky, you might be able to cash a cheque in a pub or shop. Neither did we have a phone at home at the time, so Dad had to call a neighbour and get him to pass on a message to Mum. It was 1967, but when you think of the technology we had access to, it seems like 100 years ago. We managed to get the coach home the next day, and they accepted our tickets.

Me with my Mum on Bleaberry Fell in the Lake District

That was the start of a lifelong love of the Lake District for me. Over the next 10 years, I must have visited at least 100 times and climbed almost all the fells and visited all the valleys and lakes. The only part I don't know that well is what Wainwright[27] has called the 'Far Eastern Fells'. One of my best ever trips with Dad was staying at Black Sail Youth Hostel in Ennerdale and climbing Pillar and Great Gable. The

---

[26] One pound fifty pence. It must have taken me several months to save up that amount of money.
[27] In the 1950s and 60s Alfred Wainwright wrote a series of seven guides to walking in the Lake District which have become classics and are still widely used.

hostel was a converted shepherd's bothy that slept about 10 people. It is in a fantastic location at the head of the valley, overlooked by the northern face of Great Gable, and it is the best mountain hut in England. There's nothing quite like sitting outside Black Sail Hut in the evening and watching the sun set on the mountains. It is one of the finest experiences you can have in the Lakes.

The 1960s and 70s were a time when everybody wanted everything to be very 'modern'. This was both a reaction against the gloom of postwar austerity and a sign of increasing prosperity. Nobody wanted to live in terrace houses anymore, and everybody wanted stuff that was new. We were living in the age of the 'white heat of technology'[28]. It was a time when Tomorrow's

The infamous Reliant

---

[28] From Harold Wilson's famous Labour Party conference speech in 1963. It was his first speech as Labour leader.

World[29] seemed to show startling new technological advances every week. We all assumed that there would be flying cars, ray guns, and people living on the Moon by the end of the century.

So this was an era where if you couldn't live in a new house, you had to modernise the one you were in; it was also the birth of DIY – there were no B&Qs or Do-It-Alls or out of town superstores – you bought paint, wallpaper, and all the other bits and pieces from local hardware shops in Middleton town centre. All in all, some fairly grim things were done to houses in those days and a lot of the character of the old places was lost forever. But nobody could object to new bathrooms, indoor toilets, showers, and central heating.

So, people relentlessly ripped out doors and fireplaces from older houses. Encouraged by TV stars like Barry Bucknell, the DIY man, they covered old Victorian doors with hardboard panels. Lovely old solid front doors were replaced with glass doors, iron fire places with tiled fire places, fireplaces with gas fires, and so on. We were lucky we had a new house (despite the fireplace), so we had no need to rip things out, but we had the latest wallpaper and carpets. We had

The Citroen Dyane on our trip to Skye

---

[29] Weekly BBC programme about developments in technology. Very popular at the time. The original host was Raymond Baxter who had been a Spitfire pilot in WWII.

some pretty weird 70s wallpaper. We used to have this stuff with bright orange and purple squares on it in a brick wall-like pattern. At least my Mum and Dad managed to avoid brown which became ubiquitous in the 70s as anybody who has ever watched 'Terry and June' or 'Whatever happened to the Likely Lads' would know. Terry and June had brown carpets, brown settee, brown curtains, etc. Terry wore brown trousers and brown cardigan – I kid you not! Check out some 1970s TV sitcoms and shows.

One thing that is worth mentioning is how the attitude to kids has changed. I'm not suggesting that parents didn't care about their children, but, particularly in the company of adults, children were expected to be respectful and quiet. "Children should be seen and not heard" was a refrain I experienced on a number of occasions. Nowadays, children are largely the centre of attention.

Eventually, in about 1970, the inescapable happened – Dad's infamous three-wheeler gave up the ghost. It happened in fairly dramatic fashion one evening when we were coming back from visiting some friends of my parents, Bob and Sheila, who lived in an old farmhouse in Warburton. At a roundabout, Dad was about

Me at the dining room table with the microscope my Dad bought me

to take a left when the old jalopy came shuddering to a halt. Years of care had failed to prevent the inevitable decay. Analysis showed that the front chassis had collapsed due to rust! While Dad cursed, I crossed my fingers – the RAC man confirmed the diagnosis was fatal! A few days later, Dad appeared in a car with four wheels! – but it was a Citroen Dyane![30] The Dyane was followed by two Citroen 2CVs until eventually Dad got a proper four-wheel car, a Vauxhall estate when I was about 15. It came a bit late, but the years of torment were over!

It's worth a mention of our trip to Skye in the Citroen Dyane. It was a long journey, and we'd only been there a couple of days when a car coming in the opposite direction threw up a stone which shattered our windscreen. My Dad drove to the nearest phonebox and looked

This is me looking at the Old Shambles in Manchester

---

[30] Big sister of the legendary Citroen 2CV. The Dyane was 600cc and like the 2CV (400cc!) had a canvas roof, windows that lifted up and a gear lever on the dash.

up local garages. There were none that could replace a Citroen windscreen. In fact, the nearest was in Glasgow! We did manage to find a garage that could fit us a temporary plastic windscreen which had to do us until we got home.

Speaking of the old three-wheeler, my Dad spent a lot of time on maintenance. He was often to be found in our driveway complete with the boiler suit covered in oil. It was much more usual for people to fix their own cars in those days. While this was done mainly to save money, and also because many men enjoyed messing with cars, it was easier and cheaper to do your own repairs in the days before electronic engine management systems and computer chips.

The end of the Reliant was the end of an era. Now, we had a proper car, telephone, and colour TV! – Dad even bought a stereo to replace the old Decca phonogram – the white heat of technology had at last reached No. 86 Warwick Road!

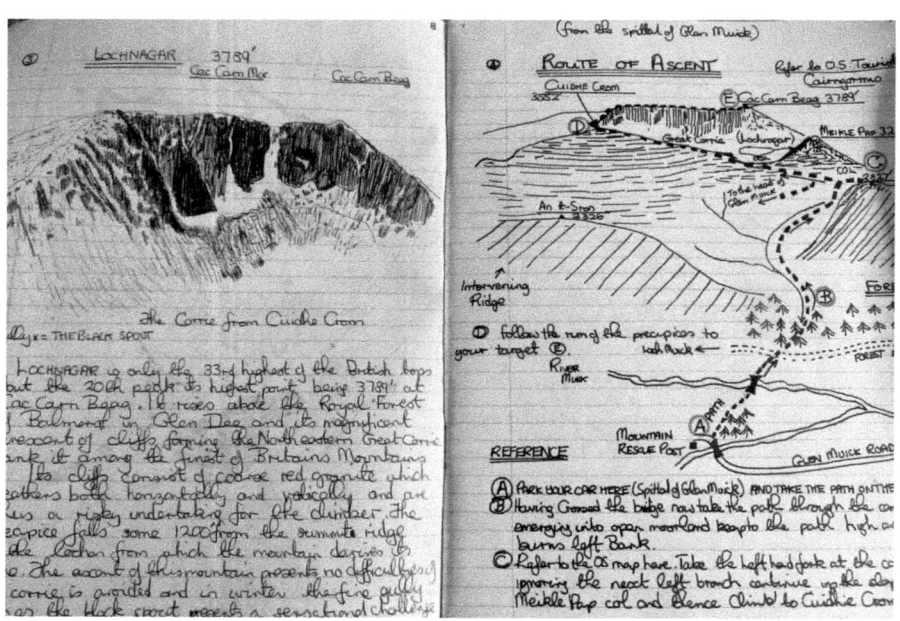

I was a huge fan of Alfred Wainwright and in my early teens I made my own walking guidebook

Chapter 5
JUNIOR SCHOOL

Mum taught me to read and write before I went to school. This created a problem for me because I had not been taught in the 'approved way' at the time. Teachers at school seemed to be annoyed that I'd been taught to read at all! Reading pretty quickly became an obsession once I got the hang of it. Before I went to school proper, I went to a nursery school for a while. My Dad used to take me on his Honda 90, and although I can't remember where the nursery was, it wasn't far from where we lived in Alkrington. I didn't like the place and would much rather have been back home with my Mum and friends. The crunch came when I was told I had to eat a bowl of Heinz spaghetti and ended up tipping it over this bloke who worked there. That was my first real rebellion and the end of that nursery school for me.

The starting day at the infant's school was up 'til then the most traumatic event of my life. I was one of those kids who had to be dragged to school kicking and screaming. It's a faintly embarrassing recollection now, but I was having far too much fun with my mates at home to want to spend my time sitting behind a desk in a poxy old school. I wasn't exactly Bart Simpson, but school was an imposition on my valuable time! The school was Alkrington County Primary School, and the Head was a guy called Mr Kirk, who I remember as a fairly kindly chain-smoking Scotsman with nicotine-stained fingers[31]. Other teachers who taught me were Mr Durham and Mrs Jones.

At lower school, we used to do reading and writing and basic maths like addition and subtraction and learn our times table[32]. We did things like standing up at our desks and trying to count up to a hundred. This

---

[31] Another sign of the times. I had a nicotine stained finger when I smoked roll-ups in the late 70s. Nicotine stained fingers were not uncommon in heavy smokers - how many do you see nowadays?

[32] Our school 'times table' used to go up to 12 x 12. Pocket electronic calculators weren't developed 'til the 1970s. One of the first available ones in the UK was the Sinclair Cambridge which retailed for £29.95 a huge sum in those days probably about as expensive as buying a laptop today.

was really difficult to do at the time without making a mistake. When we got older, we moved on to 'long' multiplication and division and calculations in old money – good old pounds, shillings, and pence.

In some classrooms, there were tables at which you could sit four children, but higher up the school, the desks we had were the old fashioned single ones with a lid that lifted up and that you could keep books in. Each one had a hole in the top right hand side for an inkwell. Most of the desks had ceramic pots in the inkwell hole, but we had modern technology – the biro! These were made of thick plastic and always used to make smudges no matter how neat you tried to be.

The good old 12x table

	1	2	3	4	5	6	7	8	9	10	11	12
1	1	2	3	4	5	6	7	8	9	10	11	12
2	2	4	6	8	10	12	14	16	18	20	22	24
3	3	6	9	12	15	18	21	24	27	30	33	36
4	4	8	12	16	20	24	28	32	36	40	44	48
5	5	10	15	20	25	30	35	40	45	50	55	60
6	6	12	18	54	30	36	42	48	54	60	66	72
7	7	14	21	28	35	42	49	56	63	70	77	84
8	8	16	24	32	40	48	56	64	72	80	88	96
9	9	18	27	36	45	54	63	72	81	90	99	108
10	10	20	30	40	50	60	70	80	90	100	110	120
11	11	22	33	44	55	66	77	88	99	110	111	122
12	12	24	36	48	60	72	84	96	108	120	122	144

Our classrooms all had one complete wall, which was windows, and you had to use a pole with a hook on to open the top ones. The windows looked out onto the school playing fields, and in the summer, the sun used to blaze through them mercilessly. This was where we used to have school sports day with egg and spoon races (not real eggs), tug of war, and a sack race. Sack races are always good fun because there is a definite technique which some people (myself included) never seem to master and hence fall flat on their faces. In the 'big' school, we used to play football and cricket on the playing field and rounders in the school playground. Rounders was never regarded as a girl's game at our school, and it was 'cool' to be good at rounders if you were a boy.

My old favourite was the school times table. It had to be learnt off by heart because we were tested on it regularly. How many times have I repeated this? I must have done it at least 100 times.

Other things that stick in my mind are cutting paper with those small blunt scissors, Gloy paste, Copydex, poster paints, crepe paper, HB pencils, and lots of chalk and talk. We always seemed to be cutting, pasting, and drawing things. Copydex was a white rubbery glue which you could make into little balls which would bounce like a mini super ball. Proper super balls, which were very hard rubber and bounced really high when you threw them, were really popular at that time. We had hours of fun with it.

In the gym, there were ropes, wall-bars, benches, beanbags, and parquet flooring. The girls always used to wear navy blue PE (physical education) knickers. We had to take what were called pump bags on 'games' days.[33] These were a bit like duffle bags made of cloth, with a drawstring, usually made by your Mum. Everything used to have a label on it with your name on. The pump bags were kept on hooks with coats on the school cloakroom. We used to have favourite games that we would play during gym time like 'pirates'. In this game, you were chased by someone who was 'on'. You could only try to escape by using benches, wall-bars, and ropes; that is, you couldn't touch the floor. If you touched the floor or were 'tagged', you were 'out' of the game. The last one 'out' was usually the next one 'on'. It was great, and we always had a really good laugh.

In the playground, it was kids' games, hide and seek, running around, and kicking a football, while the girls used to play hopscotch, and used skipping ropes and hop, skip, and jump. At one time, there was a Dalek craze, and we all used to go round shouting "exterminate!" There was the usual amount of boisterousness and fighting. We used to play lots of hide and seek or 'tag' type games. We also told a lot of jokes, most we had learned from our parents or seen on TV. In those days, everybody told jokes. Unfortunately, some were racist and sexist, but at that age, we didn't know any better. Some

---

[33] The pump bags used to contain gym kit including pumps (or plimsolls as they were sometimes called). There were no 'trainers' then.

jokes were one-liners, and most were fairly brief and terrible along the lines of: "Why are Penguins afraid of coming to Britain? Because they don't like to be near Wales".

I need to mention school milk. We used to get a bottle every day. I was a third of a pint, and we used to drink it through a straw. It was delivered in crates and used to be warm in the summer and freezing cold in the winter. This was ended in the 70s by Margaret Thatcher – 'The Milk Snatcher!'.

In my final year, I was given the cane by Mr Kirk for fighting in the toilets – we weren't actually fighting, just messing about – but since we were caught for the second time in the same day, it didn't seem worth arguing. The cane, which was literally a short piece of cane, was given on the palm of the hand. Who were the other culprits? I can't remember. For me, it was a real shock, not the actual caning, but the fact that I'd been caned in the last few days at junior school after being there for 6 years!

Apart from lessons on RE (religious education), English, maths, and bits of history, art, PE, and geography, we used to get taught things like road safety – "look right, look left and look right again .... if it's all clear walk across – don't run!" – and had something called the Tufty Club. Tufty was a very sensible squirrel with whom we were meant to identify, though the roads were a lot less busy in those days. We used to take our cycling proficiency tests when we were about nine, and if you passed, you got a pennant that you could attach to your bike. Now, where is my pennant I wonder? I wish I still had it.

Fortunately, the school was only about 15 or so minutes walk from where I lived – down Warwick Road, Gloucester Road and Kingsway[34]. The first time I went on my own I was probably about seven or eight. Nobody worried about young kids walking to school alone. The one busy road I had to cross had a Lollipop lady. Whether my Mum used to come and collect me in the winter when it was dark or not I can't recall. But I don't think she did. There was concern at the time about kids going to and from school in the dark and getting run over, and some kids, including me, used to wear reflective bands, so they could be seen more easily.

---

[34] Not so many problems with the 'school run' in those days.

Junior School

One big change for me now is that the days seemed so long at that time – I can remember lovely long summer days, and summer holidays for 6 weeks that seemed to go on forever – fabulous! In term time, I used to gaze out of the classroom windows onto the school playing field and daydream about the coming school holidays.

There was one thing I avoided at school, and that was the dreaded chickenpox. In those days, there were chickenpox parties where parents tried to get their children to catch the virus because it was reckoned to be less severe in children than adults. I remember going to school and being the only one in the classroom. I'm still hoping I will never get it. I did however catch German measles (Rubella) and came out in a rash.

Strangely enough, I never had any really big mates at junior school, at least not until the last couple of years. This was mainly because I socialised all the time with the kids on my street. A lot of the other kids at my school lived on the other side of Alkrington which seemed a long way off at that time. Apart from Beverly and Alison, who were below me at school, Terry, Julie, and co. were all Catholic and went to a different school. Friends I remember well are Peter Foden, Stephen

Playing football at junior school. I'm at the back

Grimmer, and Robin Brown. There were also a couple of girls I flirted with in my final year – Jane Shorrocks and Yvonne Rusby.

When I got a bit older and began to travel further afield in Alkrington, I started to develop friendships with other kids who had been in my class but ended up going to the same Grammar school as me. This was mainly down to my bike, always my best possession when I was a kid; I used to ride miles on it.

Old School photo
Alkrington County Primary School – Class of 1968

Left to right. Back Row: Simon Croydon, Robert Hartley, Peter Little, Elizabeth Abbot, Anne Greaves, Deborah Foster, Margaret Hallworth, Martin Reddin, Phillip Gibson, Ian Schofield. Second Row: Colin Wheatley, Alex Cross, Graham Steinsberg, Martin Williams, David Clayton, Malcom Grant, Phillip Wood, Howard Parkinson. Third Row: David Bottomley, Peter Bottomley, Martin Kaye, Stephen Grimmer, Stephen Fisher, Nicholas kay, Robin Brown, Hugh Pierce-Jones, Ian Jenkins.and Howard Thorp. Front Row: Vivien Fletcher, Anne Jones, Denise Molyneux, Susan Henshall, Gillian Sutherland, Jayne Shorrocks, Yvonne Rusby, Hilary Nichols

Chapter 6
FREEZING WINTERS AND LONG HOT SUMMERS

In the 60s, there seemed to be a considerable amount of snow and freezing cold weather – something which gradually began to disappear in the 70s and 80s. Nobody mentioned climate change to me then. We didn't have full central heating in our house at the time despite the fact that it was built in 1960. Nor were we connected for gas. We had a coal fire in the lounge which heated a boiler for hot water which supplied several radiators and an immersion tank with an electric heater. Bags of coal were delivered weekly by the coalman in his truck, and Dad had to empty the sacks into our coal bunker.

So, we had the coal bunker in the back garden, soot and smoke, and fireguards, though I don't ever remember the chimney being swept it must have been. Of course, as soon as I was old enough, I used to love lighting the fire and remember getting up to light it in the morning at weekends. The house must have been fairly well insulated despite the fact that double glazing was unusual at the time because I can't remember it being very cold at home most of the time – except for cold feet which I still suffer from – although then it was common for people to wear jumpers and cardigans indoors. When it was very cold, we used to get ice on the inside of windows in my bedroom and hot water bottles were much used.

As soon as decent snow appeared – which seemed to happen every year in the 60s – it was time to get making a snowman. There is a definite technique to this, and much depends on the quality of the snow. It's no wonder the Eskimos have twenty words for it. You want fresh snow preferably at least three inches deep, four or five is probably better, and it needs to be the 'sticky' type, that is, not dry and powdery. You start by making an ordinary snowball of the type used for throwing and then roll it in unspoilt snow. You need to begin rolling somewhere near where you want the snowman to end up; a large lawn is fairly good if the grass underneath is short.

As you roll, the ball will pick up snow rapidly and get bigger, and you need to keep turning it as you roll to get a rounded shape rather than a cylinder. Of course, it soon gets heavy and how big a ball you can roll depends on how strong you are. Towards the end, stop turning to get more of a cylindrical (torso) shape. By now, it's hard to move and you'll need to lift it so it stands on one end. If you can make one three to four foot high, you are doing pretty well. Now you have the body, a smaller rounded ball which can be lifted up will do for the head. Coal is used for the eyes and mouth, and you need to blag a carrot off your Mum for the nose. If you really want to go to town, add an old hat or scarf[35]. Now you have made a pretty good snowman which should last for days if it keeps cold. You can see me on the front cover in my duffle coat with one of my many snowmen.

Apart from snowball fighting, the next best thing with snow is sledging and sliding. We used to make slides along an even length of pavement until the snow was packed down hard like ice. With a bit of luck, you can get a slide maybe 20–30 foot long, if there is a bit of a slope – all the better. Once you have the snow packed down and smooth, you can get up quite a good speed on the slide. Eventually, you end up sliding on pure ice. Sliding was always a slightly precarious pastime and the source of plenty of rips, grazes, and freezing toes.

The best slope for sledging where I lived was at Alkrington Hall – the once home of the Lees family, and the nearest thing we had to a proper stately home locally. The hall, which was owned by the council, was at the top of a hill overlooking the southern part of Middleton and Rhodes. A long sweeping slope came down from the front of the hall which was ideal for sledging.

Dad built me a sledge out of wood. It had a very straightforward design with two large slats for runners, four or five cross pieces, and a length of rope for pulling back uphill. It was a one-man sledge, though we used to cram two on sometimes. There was little need for waxing the runners or adding metal because the snow was usually of a good enough quality for it to work well. Few people had shop-bought sledges, but the ones that did mostly had sledges with a metal frame

---

[35] I've added this degree of detail in the ancient art of snowman making in case in these days of global warming, the art is lost.

Snow in Warwick Road. Our house is on the extreme right

and runners with a wooden platform on top. Plastic sledges of the type used now were unheard of at the time.

One of the other attractions at Alkrington Hall was Pessagno's Ice Cream. The dairy was at the back of the Hall, and I was never tired of eating their ice creams and loved the 99s. They had one or two old vans which toured Alkrington on a regular basis throughout the year, and I always looked forward to them coming down our street. Speaking of coming down our street, I must mention the rag and bone man. I can't remember his name, but this was real Steptoe and Son stuff. He trundled down our street with his horse drawn wagon shouting "Ragbone! Ragbone!". Great stuff! Also, a shout out to the binmen in flat caps and donkey jackets, who collected our rubbish contained in metal dustbins.

At junior school, the long six week summer break seemed to go on for ever. I'd be up early on summer mornings and play all day in the street with friends. Warwick Road was pretty quiet traffic-wise, particularly during the day, so we had the whole thing to ourselves. As far as the gang was concerned, our end of the street was 'our' patch. Kids from further down the road didn't play on our part of the street, and we didn't mix with them often, except when playing particular games which usually happened in the evening after tea. These games were usually restricted to summer evenings when it was dry and light late.

Sledging at Alkrington Hall

We used the road for the games – sometimes pretending the road was a river. We'd get 8 to 10 kids playing games like "Cat and mouse", "Blind man's buff", "May I?", "Crocodile", or "Farmer, Farmer" – "Farmer, Farmer may I cross your golden river". These games were a variation on a theme where one person was "on" and the other had to sneak across the road and "tag" him or her without getting spotted. Movement was restricted to various kinds of steps each with their own name and rules. For example, for an "umbrella", you had to hold an imaginary umbrella and do one twirl with it. Cheating was an accepted part of the game, and kids used to try and steal extra steps without getting caught. If you got caught, you got sent back to the start.

In Blind Man's buff, the person who was 'on' was blindfolded with a scarf. They then had to stretch their arms out and try to catch one of the other players who would call out and dance around the blind man trying to avoid his touch..

Me with Alison and Beverly enjoying a cooling drink in the summer

We used to play the usual games such as football and cricket but not so much while still at primary school. Football didn't get played so often because of the high proportion of girls in the gang and most girls didn't play football then. One game we played combined a football and hide and seek, and we called it "Kitcan" (Kickcan). The idea was that you would place a football in the middle of the road and someone, usually one of the older boys, would kick it as hard as they could down the street. While the person who was 'on' chased after the ball, and returned it to the spot, the others would all go and hide. The person who was on had to catch the others, but they could be freed if someone who hadn't been caught could sneak up and kick the ball away. The person 'on' always had to be looking after their shoulder to guard the ball as well as find the others. Our games used to go on late into summer evenings until we got called in one by one.

We played with skipping ropes and roller stakes, dressed as cowboys and Indians, and had battles with toy pistols and bows and arrows. We also built bogie carts from old prams.

At the back of Hardfield Road, which was roughly parallel to our street, there was what I remember as being the only remaining farm in Alkrington. It lay between our estate and the River Irk. There was a pond by the roadside, and we used to go with our nets and jam jars and collect tadpoles, frogs, and sticklebacks, some of which ended up in the small pond in our back garden. At the time, the Irk was heavily polluted and usually frothing with foam on the surface. You wouldn't have wanted to fall in! I learnt to swim breaststroke when I was five, but I've never been a particularly strong swimmer. We were pretty careful, but one of the dangerous things we did do was tunnel into a sandbank by the river to make a hide away. We had great fun doing it, and fortunately, it didn't collapse. Nobody got buried.

In our back garden with my friend Peter

From an early age, I had a tricycle and then graduated to a proper bike; a red Vindec Pavemaster was my first ever proper bike. When it came, my Dad had put stabilisers on it, but I soon got beyond those. I spent many happy hours riding that bike. It gave me a sense of freedom and was always good exercise. As I got older, I travelled further afield in Alkrington visiting some of my other friends from junior school who lived near Mainway. This proved to be good because some of them went on to attend the same Grammar school as me.

Chapter 7
CULTURE

I used to go to the local branch library in Alkrington near the shops at the top of Mainway, and I rapidly read my way through the children's section. I loved lots of authors including Alan Garner, who I thought was quite magical[36], C S Lewis, and Joan Aiken. My top books for a long time were the Swallows and Amazons adventure stories by Arthur Ransome. I used to daydream that I was sailing on that lake on many a hot summer afternoon. I used to become almost completely immersed in the story and felt like I was there with Nancy, Peggy, John, Susan, Titty, Roger, and Captain Flint.

One of the things I loved about those books was the way the children were so self-sufficient with map reading, sailing, camping, signalling, and secret codes. At that time, in the mid 60s, those books were already 30 years old but still credible. It was only in the early 70s that nylon tents, rucksacks, and cagoules became available; many people then used canvas tents and rucksacks and walking boots that hadn't changed much in design or style since the 30s. To kids brought up today with computer games, satellite navigation, and mobile phones, the Swallows and Amazons stories must seem like ancient history, and sadly, it's easy to see why they don't have quite the same appeal.

When I was about nine, I discovered The Hobbit by J R R Tolkien and went on to read Lord of the Rings, my top book well into my teens. Later, I recorded in my diary on 8 February 1969 how I went on the number 17 bus (Rochdale to Manchester), caught from the bottom of Mainway, to Manchester and bought the original paperback edition of Lord of the Rings for 30 shillings[37]. My first trip to the centre of Manchester on my own – I can remember feeling very grown up!

By the time I was starting at secondary school, I was travelling regularly to the main local library on Long Street in Middleton,

---

[36] I still do. I was lucky enough to see him speak a few years ago and have recently finished reading Treacle Walker.
[37] £1.50 in new money. You could have bought about 10 pints of bitter for that amount of money.

opposite the Old Boar's Head Pub. It seemed very grown up and serious stuff going to Middleton library, rather than Alkrington library, and I can recall how big, dark, and quiet it seemed. For me, this was a treasure trove, and I spent many happy hours there. It was then I'd started reading books by John Wyndham, such as Day of the Triffids and The Midwich Cuckoos, and C S Forester's Hornblower books, Sherlock Holmes by Arthur Conan Doyle, and H G Wells The War of The Worlds.

I went on to read books by George Orwell, Gavin Maxwell, Harper Lee, J D Salinger, and Graham Greene. I was mad about books and had no doubt at the time that one day I would be a famous author! Sherratt and Hughes[38] in St Anne's Square was the Manchester Mecca for books at that time, and I spent many happy hours and most of my carefully collected spending money in there. I used to enjoy travelling on the old buses. There was no door, and you could jump on and off. Smokers were confined to upstairs, and the popular seats were at the top front from where you had a good view.

Of course, I didn't just enjoy reading; I also loved writing and wrote some poems and a book. The book, called Farkendal and the Ice Lord, was about the adventures of a Gandalf-like wizard. He had a "purple beard (the longest in the village), a long nose, and mischievous green eyes". It was very derivative of my favourite writers Garner, Lewis, and Tolkien. I managed four chapters totalling 57 pages and a map of the Wild lands of the North. If only I had finished it. Maybe I will one day.

I wrote about 50 poems. Sadly, most of them have been lost, but here are just a few of my remaining gems:

The Man On The Cloud

The window in my bedroom
Is near the door
On a clear starry night
You can see Patrick Moore

---

[38] Alas it is now W H Smiths.

The Man With The Mouth

The man with the mouth
Makes all sound
Startles crowd
Shakes the ground
Waxes lyrical
Waning never
He also thinks
He's very clever.

Soliloquy

This life of ours
The good, the bad
Crying
Laughing
Happy
Mad
Enclosed in the prison
Of our minds
Each searching for a freedom
One never really finds

Learned Feet

I walk through corridors and cloisters
Where learned feet have trud
And here, having learnt something at least
Step lightly, beware the crud
The quiet here is one of scholarly contemplation
Philosophy, classics, science and politics of the nation

And now I gaze amazed
At pine tables old, and passages windswept cold
Not empty but filled with ghosts
Of Einstein, Plato, DaVinci, thinkers for the most
And in empathy with their dismay
I turn my feet away
Into the brightness of a brand new day

The book and poems were all written between the ages of about 9 to 14. Why didn't I continue? The simple answer is science. By about 14, I had decided that I was going to be a research scientist and find a cure for cancer. I've started writing poems now and again as a kind of therapy. Writing a poem is a mindfulness moment for me.

Before I was a teenager, I didn't used to listen to the radio, or should I say wireless, much apart from on Saturday mornings when Ed Stuart was on. In those days, we had three radio stations, the Light Programme (Radio 2), the Third Programme (Radio 3), and the Home Service (Radio 4). We also had Radio Luxembourg and the pirate station Radio Caroline, which operated from a ship in the North Sea. Eventually, the BBC woke up to the fact that there was a real demand for pop music, created Radio 1, and reorganised its programming, making stars of people like Tony Blackburn.

My Mum used to have the radio on all of the time in the kitchen during the day. The kitchen was her domain. I used to hear 'Listen with Mother' with her when I was younger. We also listened to some of the classics such as The Archers, Desert Island Discs, Just a Minute with the inimitable Nicholas Parsons who hosted for over 50 years, and I'm Sorry I Haven't a Clue – the antidote to panel games, chaired by the legendary Humphrey Lyttelton, and with Graeme Garden, Barry Cryer, and Tim Brooke-Taylor[39].

My Dad, who was always trying to interest me in science (and usually succeeded), helped me make a crystal radio set. It had a coil which was made of wire wrapped around a toilet roll tube and a wire aerial that stretched from my bedroom window all the way down the garden. I used to lie in bed at night, listening in with headphones and trying to find as many stations as possible.

Television was the biggest single influence on all us kids. Pre-school, it was the Woodentops – "the spottiest dog you ever did see!", Andy Pandy, The Flower Pot Men, and Tales from the Riverbank – a bizarre series of adventures involving real mice, guinea pigs, etc., zooming around in toy boats on a fairly crappy set – oddly enough – the wee beasts didn't seem to mind! By Junior school, it was Dr Who with William Hartnell always my number one Doctor – and yes of

---

[39] The host and participants may have changed but all of these programmes can still be found on BBC Radio 4.

course, I did hide behind the settee the first time the Daleks appeared on our black and white telly. Despite the grainy pictures and wobbly sets, Dr Who really gripped its audience. We just hadn't really seen anything like that on TV before, and the superb BBC radiophonic workshop theme written by Ron Grainer, and realised by Delia Derbyshire, added a genuinely sinister edge to the proceedings. It was thrilling to hear. Groundbreaking stuff!

Later, when I was a bit older, my favourite programme was The Man From UNCLE – with Napoleon Solo and Ilya Kuryakin – which I was allowed to stay up late to see. Although this was obviously a spoof, I can recall taking it dead seriously – I sent off to the BBC for my Man From UNCLE badge and Dad bought me a Luger as used by Illya Kuryakin. I used to spend ages playing at being spies with my mates on our road.

Like most kids then and ever since,[40] I was straight home from school and in parked front of the telly. The early evening kids programmes used to include Blue Peter, Magpie, Fireball XL5 – a great favourite of mine I even had the Airfix kit – Vision On with Tony Hart, Crackerjack with Leslie Crowther, Thunderbirds, Stingray, and Captain Scarlet. Then there was that great five minute slot before the six o'clock news in which we enjoyed Tin Tin, The Magic Roundabout, Pogles Wood, Noggin the Nog, Captain Pugwash, The Herbs, Clangers, Hectors House, and most of the other best ever programmes on telly. If ever there was a slot that needed reviving, that is it! bring it back!

Blue Peter was the flagship BBC programme for kids back then. It was very popular and loved by millions including me. We were glued to the telly watching Christopher Trace, Valerie Singleton, Peter Purves, John Noakes, and Shep the border collie dog. It began in 1958 and is still running. We were treated to making all sorts of useful things out of the legendary 'sticky backed plastic' and old washing up liquid bottles, followed by "here's one I made earlier". Then there was the Blue Peter garden and the famous badges which you could get if you appeared on the show or achieved something notable. Alas, I never got one, but I've heard they are for sale on eBay. I can

---

[40] Oops!, this has dated a bit since I wrote it. I expect tablets and mobiles have probably taken over.

still remember clearly the legendary episode when they had Lulu the baby elephant on the show, who pooped all over the set, much to the embarrassment of the presenters, and her keeper.

These times were the heyday of 'light entertainment', with shows hosted by celebrities like Des O'Connor, Bruce Forsyth, and Bob Monkhouse. The hosts cracked gags, sang, and introduced guests who were often comedians or singers, and included stars like Shirley Bassey and Mariane Faithfull. So, for the grown-ups, it was things like Saturday Night at the London Palladium, Morecambe and Wise, Billy Cotton, and The Black and White Minstrel Show – so called light entertainment with blackface! But there were also classics like The Avengers, The Likely Lads, 'Til Death Us Do Part, The Prisoner, Porridge, Monty Pythons Flying Circus – probably my favourite ever comedy show – Dixon of Dock Green, Z Cars, and Coronation Street. Naturally, a lot of this was in black and white on a slightly snowy screen some of the time.

There were comedy sketch shows with great performers who had us all laughing, including Tommy Cooper, Spike Milligan, Michael Bentine, Kenneth Williams, Les Dawson, Harry Worth, Tony Hancock, and The Two Ronnies (Barker and Corbett) – "It's goodnight from me and its goodnight from him". I have to put in a special mention for Spike Milligan here. My Dad was a massive fan. He loved to listen to the Goon Shows in the 1950s and bought me the book of the scripts. Although the Goon Show was really before my time, I enjoyed reading Spike's books, including Adolf Hitler My Part In His Downfall, Puckoon, and others. I also loved watching him on TV in the 60s and 70s, in shows such as Q5. He was a great inspiration to many comedians including the Monty Python crew.

There were also a fair number of American TV shows we watched that were very popular, including Star Trek – with Captain James T Kirk and the unequalled Spock – Bewitched, and Perry Mason, starring Raymond Burr. There were also more serious current affairs programmes like Panorama and interviews by people like David Frost on the Frost Programme. Frost started out in satire in the early 1960s with the legendary That Was the Week That Was. His most famous interviews were with American ex-president Richard Nixon in 1977.

I need to make a quick mention of the classic adverts of those decades. The ones that stick with me are "A Double Diamond works wonders, works wonders, A Double Diamond works wonders, so buy one today!" – and, as I found out, it was a good pint for its time! Then there was the all time classic 'Go to Work on an Egg!' From none other than the Egg Marketing Board (yes, there was such a thing) with a classic advert featuring Tony Hancock and Patricia Hayes. Finally who could possibly forget doing the "Shake and Vac'.

When I was born, there were two channels – BBC and ITV – which were launched in 1955. A third channel, BBC2, started in 1967 and was the first British channel to carry programmes in colour. At this time, I was lucky enough to have a friend called Robin, who lived on Mainway in Alkrington, whose parents had a colour TV set. This was pretty well unheard of at the time, and there could only have been a few thousand in the country. It cost about £500. I can remember it being huge (most tellies were big in those days anyway – no flat screen!) and having three knobs to control the colour, one for blue, red, and green. Most of the time test films were shown on BBC2 in preparation for proper broadcasting, things like 'How Steel is Made'. I can remember being completely transfixed watching the miracle of colour telly and twiddling the three knobs to get the best colour picture.

There was no daytime TV, and if you switched the TV on before about four o'clock, there was a 'test card' being shown. The test card had a series of lines on it and helped you to get the best picture by adjusting things like the 'vertical' and 'horizontal hold', which were all important on tellies in those days.

Probably, the highlight of my telly watching life occurred on 20 July 1969 when Apollo 11 landed on the Moon. This happened round about midnight GMT, so it must have been the early hours of the 20th, and I got to stay up late and watch. Luckily for me, my Dad was as excited about it as I was (my Mum however went to bed). It's hard to describe what an incredible experience it was watching the glow of grey, grainy pictures of Neil Armstrong making the first tentative steps on the moon – "One small step for a man, one giant leap for mankind". Looking back, it almost seems like something out of an H G Wells novel. The excitement as Dad and I sat around the TV was intense. We were witnessing what was possibly the greatest ever human achievement taking place live from our own living room! Just before the landing started, there was a knock on the front door

"Who the hell is that at this hour?" said my Dad going to investigate. It was the next door neighbour in his dressing gown and slippers, who hadn't got at TV, coming round to share the experience. When you think of the technology they had in those days, it was amazing they got there and back in one piece.

Second only to this was England winning the World Cup in 1966. I sat and watched that whole game live from Wembley, in black and white, completely spellbound. The whole country was caught up in the festive mood that we had done so well. The pubs were full, and we all celebrated. Equal second was Manchester United winning the European Cup in 1968. Pictures of George Best, Bobby Charlton, and Brian Kidd scoring goals are etched in my mind – even more so than the world cup goals. Moments like that are very special and worth treasuring throughout your life.

Apart from the Vietnam War and the Troubles (more on this later), three of the worst things I ever saw on the telly were Aberfan, the assassination of president JF Kennedy, and the the death of Donald Campbell. JFK, as he was known, was killed in Dallas, Texas, in 1963. He was shot by Lee Harvey Oswald as he was passing by the book depository in a motorcade.

The Aberfan disaster was the catastrophic collapse of a colliery spoil tip into the village of Aberfan in south Wales. In October 1966, the tip slid down the mountainside and engulfed part of the village including Pantglas Junior school, killing 116 children and 28 adults. I can still remember the shock of horrid scenes in the TV news.

Donald Campbell was a British speed record breaker who broke eight world speed records on land and water in the 1950s and 60s. His speed vehicles were called Bluebird, and he inherited the first from his father, Sir Malcolm Campbell, who was a world speed record holder in the 1920s and 30s. In attempting to set a new water speed record in January 1967 on Coniston Water in the Lake District, he was killed when Bluebird lifted off the surface of the water and did an almost complete backflip. His body was finally found in 2000. I know Coniston well, and whenever I visit, I think of him.

How good was 1960's telly compared to now? Pretty good I would say – the absence of reality TV was wonderful. The fact that there were only three channels certainly didn't matter much to us at the time. Nobody was clamouring for more. We had a pretty good mix of dramas, documentaries, and comedies. But there were some low points. Even when I was about eight, I could see that the Black and White Minstrel Show was a pile of tosh. But there were truly great TV programmes the like of which we just don't have any more – 'Til Death Us Do Part' was a classic example of groundbreaking TV which inflamed, delighted, enraged, and divided the country – it was watched by millions of people and talked about on buses and in the workplace in a way that no TV programme is these days. Johnny Speight created a work of pure genius which exposed the contradictions and hypocrisies of British life perfectly. Nobody is challenging society in popular entertainment in the same way now. Alf Garnett was racist and sexist for sure, but the point of the programme was that he was called out for it and was the butt of the joke[41].

A special mention needs to be made for Top of the Pops because this overlapped with the next main cultural influence – pop music! These were the days of Alan Freeman – "hello pop-pickers!" – and Jimmy Saville – "hello guys and gals!" (we didn't know what a monster Saville was then). In some ways, that was the golden era of DJs. Although there are many well known and wealthy DJs now, very few are household names in the way they were then – everybody in Britain in the 60s had heard of Tony Blackburn from Radio One. Naturally enough, everybody was Beatle mad, including grannies in the early days when they were all suits and smiles[42]. And how about seeing the Stones, Beatles, Beach Boys, the Kinks Jimi Hendrix et al. on Top of the Pops!

I need to include a special mention for Sandie Shaw – who I really fancied. She had three number one hits in the charts, and the final one Puppet On a String became the first British entry to win the Eurovision Song Contest in 1967. She also had a distinctive trademark as a singer[43]. Her win was a great TV event watched by millions and if I recall correctly didn't last for about five hours as it does now.

I can't finish with TV and music without lauding another classic, The Old Grey Whistle Test with Whispering Bob Harris. It was the

---

[41] I watched an episode recently and it was hard going. I'd forgotten how quite intense and racist it was. No wonder it's not shown on TV anymore. There ought to be space for a modern version bashing the anti-woke brigade though.
[42] That ended when they grew long hair and smoked dope.
[43] What was it?

late-night slot on BBC2, and I used to watch it after my parents had gone to bed. Starting in 1971, it was a must watch if you were into the music scene, much like listening to John Peel's late show on Radio 1. It was the antidote to chart music and featured all the great bands of the 1970s. The show continued until 1988, but I stopped watching in the early 1980s.

One of my favourite toys Dad bought me was a plastic Winfield[44] 'electric' guitar that looked a bit like a Stratocaster, and I used to thrash about to She Loves You, Help, and other great Beatles singles with a boy called Keith who lived opposite and had a small portable record player that played singles. We used to spend hours miming to Beatles singles.

In the early days, we had a Decca mono record player of the kind that came in a large box with a fake crocodile skin cover. When you opened the lid, you were able to play 45s or LPs and it had a device whereby you could stack half a dozen singles and play them one after the other. My Mum and Dad had similar tastes in music and liked Frank Sinatra, Stan Getz, Dave Brubeck, Nat King Cole, and some classical music. The classical music was well known stuff by composers like Tchaikovsky, Beethoven, Sibelius, and Elgar. The first record I ever 'bought' was the Karelia Suite by Sibelius on a Decca EP. Mr Durham, a teacher at junior school, was gobsmacked because he played it in one of his lessons and only I recognised it. Although I loved music, I had very few records because most of the 'spends' I accumulated went on books – they were always the first priority. My most loved piece of music at the time was the Enigma Variations by Elgar. I used to sit in the lounge on a Saturday afternoon to listen to my favourite classical music and read a book. As a result, some books and music will always be linked for me. I listened to the Enigma Variations when I first read Coot Club by Arthur Ransome. Every time I hear it now, I think of sailing on the Norfolk Broads.

One of the best LPs I ever bought was Sgt Pepper's Lonely Hearts Club Band, and I'm pleased to say I've still got it – the original version. I rapidly moved on from that to Jethro Tull, Genesis, Pink Floyd, and Van Der Graaf Generator. I used to think Peter Hammill's solo album

---

[44] Winfield was a brand name for Woolworths.

'The Silent Corner and the Empty Stage' was just about the best bit of 'rock' music ever written. Now I'm not quite so sure, but even if it isn't, it can't be far off. Later in life, as a teenager, I got bored with Prog (progressive) Rock and really got into punk and new wave. My fave bands were The Clash, Ian Drury and the Blockheads, Elvis Costello, Television, Blondie, and Talking Heads.

When I was about eight, my Dad bought me a tape recorder. It was a Toshiba and ran on batteries. It had a separate plug in microphone. This was pre-cassette days and took small reel to reel tapes. I was fascinated by this and used to spend ages recording all sorts of sounds, putting them together and speeding them up and slowing down. The tape didn't last very long and was soon superseded replaced by a Phillips cassette player. Both of these were mono, but it's amazing how much use I got out of the cassette player. I took it everywhere.

A top pastime for us kids was to collect chewing gum cards. You used to be able to collect a set of signed black and white pictures of the Beatles. I'd imagine those would be worth something nowadays. Other notable card collections of my youth included the American Civil War series – really gruesome scenes from battles plus very real looking confederate money – and the 'Outer Limits' cards which featured weird monsters from outer space and were based on the TV series. Collecting and swapping cards to get the set was a serious business in those days.

Trips to the cinema were very special treats. I came from a TV generation, and very few kids I knew went to things like Saturday matinees. This probably had something to do with the fact that there was no cinema that was near to us. Our nearest then was called 'The Avenue' at Victoria Avenue in Blackley. But even in those days, the mid 60s, it was in decline. This was well before the days of multiplexes, and most cinemas only had one screen. I went there to see Thunderball with my Mum and Dad in the days when James Bond was really something and appealed to adults as much as kids. I was thrilled by all the early Bond films with Sean Connery, my favourite being Goldfinger. I don't ever remember there being a cinema in Middleton, though there must have been one at some time. Serious trips to the pictures meant going into 'Town' (Manchester) to places like 'The Gaumont'. Nana Thomas liked taking me there, and I went to see all the 60s children's classics of the time like Dr Doolittle, Oliver, The Sword in the Stone, and of course The Sound of Music with Julie Andrews. Some cinemas, in those days, still had organists who used to play before the film and during the intermission when the usherettes used to come round and sell ice creams.

I was football mad and started to support Manchester United in the early 60s. It was a fruitful time to be a Man U fan since we won the FA Cup in 1963, League Championship in '65 and '67, and the European Cup in 1968 – the great days of Matt Busby, Bobbie Charlton, George Best, Nobby Styles, and Dennis Law. Football was very different in those days. There was no Premier League but The Championship with four divisions. The pitches were terrible, often covered in mud, and some of the tackling that went on wouldn't be countenanced these days. I can remember watching a game on Match of the Day which took place during a snow blizzard. You couldn't see the players or the ball!

Football life was not without its frustrations; however, because my Dad wasn't the least bit interested in football, he preferred Rugby Union which he had played at school; neither were the fathers of any of my closest friends! Going to Old Trafford on my own in those days was out of the question and also difficult by bus because it was on the other side of Manchester. So I had to be content with football annuals, Match of the Day, and radio reports. By the time I got to Old Trafford in 1970, United were well into a steep decline after Matt Busby retired, and we lost to Spurs 4-1! – Bobby Charlton scored a great goal, but it wasn't much consolation.

Despite my shamefully infrequent visits to the Theatre of Dreams, I have faithfully followed United from my armchair and car seat (radio) for 40 years. Irritatingly enough, none of my friends at junior school or grammar school supported United anyway; they either didn't like football – that is, were City fans, and not many of those – or supported local teams like Oldham Athletic, or were more interested in obscure sports like Speedway. Middleton suffered for the lack of a decent local football team – though it did have a very good cricket team, and in those days, there were some top overseas international players who used to play in the Lancashire league. The nearest clubs were City, United, Oldham, and Bury. At grammar school, I even used to go and watch Latics (Oldham Athletic) with my mates who were all daft enough to support Oldham[45]. I don't think I ever saw Latics win a game in half a dozen or so visits.

Finally, I have to mention shopping and how it's changed since the 1960s and 70s. Shopping then was still largely a female activity. Housewives did the weekly shopping. The early supermarkets which opened then were simply like large grocer shops with vegetables, meat, and lots of tinned food, tiny by comparison with today's stores – not the range of stuff you would find these days, and not the 'tonnes' of plastic. Food was seasonal, and some things, such as vegetables, weren't available throughout the year. There were no bank cards or cash machines. You paid in cash that you got from a bank. Now the idea of going to a bank with your bankbook and drawing out cash seems almost absurd, and in those days, you could even get to see the bank manager if you needed a loan! Of course, it follows that people were paid in cash, or possibly by cheque. The weekly pay packet usually arrived on a Friday, just in time for a night in the pub!

Shopping still wasn't really the pastime it is now in those days – not for ordinary people anyhow – it was something you had to do to get some new clothes or shoes or put food on the table. My Mum used to do most of day-to-day shopping at the local shops in Alkrington. There were also trips into Middleton or Manchester when we used to go to the bigger stores like Lewis's on Deansgate, usually at the weekends. Goods were paid for in pounds, shillings, and pence, and groceries sold in pounds and ounces and weighed on good old-fashioned scales.

---

[45] Or so I thought at the time. Nowadays I would support my local team whatever division they were in.

Chapter 8
GRAMMAR SCHOOL

One day at Primary school, we were ushered into the hall to take the Eleven Plus. At the time, I had no idea of the significance of that exam. In fact, I didn't even know it was the Eleven Plus! That was probably a good thing because it meant I had no fear of failing it. I had noticed that my final year at school had begun to get much more serious than the other years. There was talk about which school I would go to next, and my parents were obviously concerned. I ended up passing the Eleven Plus but in the end it made no difference. I went to a grammar school because I passed the entrance exam and interview.

The part of the world I lived in, south-east Lancashire, had a long tradition of grammar schools, some of which, like Manchester Grammar School, were well known throughout the country. In the late 60s, many were being replaced by comprehensive schools, and where I lived, there were 'direct grant' grammar schools supported by the state. I ended up taking entrance exams for Bury Grammar and Hulme Grammar School in Oldham. My interview at Bury Grammar didn't go as well as I'd hoped. I was asked to describe what I had done the night before and started to talk about a trip to the cinema; half way through this, I realised that the trip had happened the night before that! I became embarrassed and clammed up a bit.

So, in September 1968, I started at Hulme Grammar School, Oldham, which was about five miles from where I lived – as the crow flies – by bus nearer six. I wouldn't have been able to go there if it hadn't been a direct grant grammar school in which fees were paid by the local authority[46]. Luckily for me, there were quite a few kids from Alkrington County Primary School who went there[47], including

---

[46] Parents had to make a contribution. The sixth form was 'free'.

[47] I checked my primary school website - in 2008 there were no school leavers who went to Hulme. One went to Bury Grammar. Hulme is now an independent fee paying school. How things have changed – for the worse.

half a dozen of my classmates from junior school, so we had a school coach which took us there and back every day.

Oldham must be one of the highest towns in England. Oldham Edge, which is not far from the town centre, is about 800 feet above sea level. On the coach going to school from Middleton, it was about six miles or so, uphill all the way. The school itself, in Werneth, was on the edge of high ground with a spectacular view over the east Lancashire plain to Manchester and beyond.

One winters day, which illustrates the arctic winter conditions in Oldham in the late 60s, went like this – I caught the school bus at about 8 o'clock in the morning in light snow, and we crept slowly up Oldham Road in the darkness and heavy traffic as the snow got deeper and deeper. It was fingers-crossed that we wouldn't be able to make it to school. But we did. In my diary – for this was the 20 February 1969 – I recorded – "terrible snow storms, huge drifts. abandoned school". The snow drifts were seven to ten feet high at the school gates; I had wet socks and feet frozen like ice from the long snow slides that we made in the school driveways.

The school building was fairly grand and had been built in the 1880s. It overlooked a set of hard 'all weather' football pitches set on the edge of the hill. On a clear day, there was quite a view. You could see the CIS building[48] in Manchester from there. In winter, it was so bone-achingly cold that you had to run around as fast as you could to avoid hypothermia. I loved football, but this was a form of torture. No allowances were made; there were no undershirts, tracksuit bottoms, or wearing gloves. If you fell on the ground or got a knock, it was bloody painful, but if it had been grass, it would have frozen hard anyway. How we survived that I don't know.

On those dark short days in December, January, and February, the old school boiler groaned under the strain and we had a few welcome days off due to it packing up. Days like this were an absolute luxury because most of the kids who came from Saddleworth couldn't get to school on days of heavy snow, and some of the teachers couldn't get in either. This meant it was impossible to run a proper timetable, so we ended up having fairly lazy days where the teachers were more

---

[48] Then, the tallest building in Manchester.

interested in keeping us amused than doing any real teaching. In the science labs, we did some 'fun' experiments and kept all the Bunsen burners going to warm the place up.

The school itself was a fascinating place – although built in the 1880s, it seemed older and definitely had public school pretensions. The Great Hall with its hammer head beams, large organ pipes, stained glass windows, and plaques commemorating sporting achievements, and sacrifices in two world wars did its best to convey a faded public-school grandeur. In assembly time with teachers in their academic gowns, the whole school singing and the organ going full blast to the strains of "Gaudeamus igitur", it almost cut the mustard. Ever seen 'If'[49]?

I had to quote the Wikipedia entry for Gaudeamus igitur here:

"De Brevitate Vitae (on the Shortness of Life), perhaps more commonly known by its first words Gaudeamus igitur (therefore let us rejoice) is a song in Latin that is a popular academic commercium song in many European countries. In many modern Western nations it is sung as an anthem at University graduation ceremonies. *Despite its use as a formal graduation hymn, it is a jocular, light-hearted composition that pokes fun at university life.*"

Note the italics they are mine. I doubt if the Headmaster had thought that the song "poked fun" at academia, we would have been allowed to sing it. Gaudeamus igitur is Latin; here is the first verse and the translation:

"Gaudeamus igitur
Juvenes dum sumus
Post jucundum juventutem
Post molestam senectutem
Nos habebit humus."

Which translates as:

"Let us rejoice therefore
While we are young.
After a pleasant youth

---

[49] IF - the movie. Worth watching if you haven't seen it.

After a troublesome old age
The earth will have us."

Cheery stuff!

Although I studied Latin at school, I never troubled to try and translate this song and I think that I only understood the first two lines.

Hulme had a subterranean gym, school canteen, and cloakroom which used to smell of glue because the woodwork teacher – Nobby Clark – lurked in his rooms down there. The glue was boiled up by Nobby from animal bones – or was it the bones of missing pupils? As an eleven year old in that spooky subterranean corridor, I could almost have believed it. It wasn't quite Gormenghast, but the whole place strove to be as traditional and ancient as it possibly could. It was certainly a strange place for an 11-year-old boy forced to wear short trousers. Yes its true! – I was unlucky enough to be in the last year that the Third Form was made to wear short trousers as part of school uniform – this was subsequently abandoned after complaints from pupils and parents – too late to prevent many of us being scarred for life[50]. To make matters worse, the school uniform consisted of a cap which had concentric rings of blue and gold – about as conspicuous as you could possibly make a cap. In addition, the socks I had to wear were also blue and gold-striped. Can you picture me sneaking down Warwick Road to catch the school bus and just praying that my chums who went to the local comp wouldn't see me?

Along with the chugging radiators, wooden panelling, parquet flooring, a smell of wood polish and stale cabbage, and battered desks, we had the really scary old relics – the teachers! They were not at all like modern teachers, the types that most people come across in comprehensives[51] today. For a start, I doubt if any in those days had taken a teaching qualification – checking my old school journal for 1968/69, I can see just one Dip.Phys.Ed. – the Masters had almost all come straight from finishing their degree course at university, and about a third were from Oxbridge. In fact, to teach at such a school in those days, doing a teaching qualification would probably have been looked

---

[50] Am I exaggerating? Not much - it was humiliating – and bloody cold in winter!
[51] This was written before the New Labour and the Tories ruined the education system by introducing Academies and 'Free' Schools.

upon as either namby pamby or dangerously subversive. Being there was like playing a part in 'Carry on Teaching'.

In order to create the correct academic atmosphere, and no doubt to protect their worn tweed jackets from all-pervasive chalk dust, many of the teachers wore their academic gowns much of the time. One or two younger rebels, and safety conscious scientists, did not. Their teaching style was dominated by chalk and talk, although some more modern teaching methods were beginning to creep in, and there was plenty of practical work in science lessons. However, it may not surprise anyone to hear that there were eccentrics amongst the teaching staff and that most had nick names to match. Amongst my favourite nicknames were 'Fred Nerk', 'Rubbergob', 'Scruff Parker', and 'Batman'.

On arrival at Hulme Grammar, my first form teacher was Mr Anderson or 'Batman' – so called because he was one of the few teachers always to be seen in his gown. He was one of the younger teachers who had an aloof manner and had the knack of class control without having to exert any great effort. As a form an English teacher, I thought Batman was pretty good without being terribly inspiring.

I hadn't been at the school long before I began to fall in love with science. It wasn't just the fact that the Bunsen burners kept us warm during the winter but the fact that we could do real experiments – something I had never come across before – and burning, boiling, and blowing things up was great fun! No, I wasn't a pyromaniac; it's just that these were the days before health and safety was invented,[52] so that we used to be allowed do more dangerous experiments in Chemistry and Physics, many of which wouldn't be allowed in schools nowadays[53]. One that always sticks in my mind is heating ammonium dichromate in which the orange crystals suddenly burst into an explosion of green snake-like threads.

By the time I had reached the second year, I was well into the swing of being at the 'big' school. Now with long trousers and no longer bottom of the heap, I actually began to enjoy being there. Why

---

[52] Not that science at Hulme in those days was slack as far as safety was concerned. We had fume cupboards, glass screens and safety glasses and were admonished to behave sensibly and safely.
[53] Such as using fairly powerful radioactive sources.

was this? There were many things about the school I didn't like – uniforms, pretentiousness, too far from home, prefects, regular homework, and no girls – but in spite of this, I liked the craic, I had some good friends, and most shockingly of all, I enjoyed many of the lessons! As my friend Steve Mingle said, there was some "quality piss taking" as you will find out in due course.

PERSONAL INFORMATION

SURNAME: THORP
Other names: HOWARD GEOFFERY
Date of Birth: 23.1.57
Home Address: 86 WARWICK RD
ALKRINGTON
MIDDLETON
Form: 3Z
Form Master: R N ANDERSON
House: LEES
House Master: K A HEARNE Esq MA

ALL ENTRIES IN THIS JOURNAL MUST BE IN INK.
A PIECE OF BLOTTING PAPER SHOULD BE KEPT IN IT.

THE GOVERNORS
PATRON
The Right Honourable The Lord Clitheroe,
P.C., M.A., D.L., F.S.A.
CHAIRMAN
H. C. Ogden, Esq., LL.B.
Governor Emeritus
Miss Marjory Lees
Co-optative Governors (appointed by the Board)
Harry C. Ogden Esq., LL.B.
Eric Denton, Esq., F.C.A., A.C.I.S., J.P.
Appointed by Hulme's Charity
Cyril Freear, Esq., F.A.C.C.A.
Andrew L. Brocklehurst, Esq.
Mrs. Mildred Jackson
Jack Blunn, Esq.
Miss Florence B. Brierley, J.P.
Appointed by Manchester Grammar School
Edward Haines, Esq., O.B.E., LL.M.
Appointed by Manchester High School for Girls
Mrs. Isa Wood, B.Sc.
Appointed by Manchester University
W. H. Chaloner, Esq., M.A., Ph.D.
Miss Audrey B. Cockshott, B.A.
Appointed by Lancashire County Council
County Councillor Lawrence Bell
Appointed by West Riding County Council
County Alderman Mrs. Elizabeth E. Smith, O.B.E., B.A., J.P.
Appointed by Oldham Town Council
Alderman Reginald Bailey
Alderman Allen Coop
Alderman Malcolm F. Bamford, J.P.
Councillor Anthony Sheehan
Councillor James S. Bulman
Councillor Alwyn B. McConnell
Councillor Alfred Clarke

First School Journal

To get back to the lessons, none of this is to say that the teachers were all brilliant and the lessons good – but being a grammar school, it had somehow managed to cultivate an ambience of learning as serious business – of academia. I felt like I was learning something useful and stimulating because we were pushed academically and treated, on the whole, like intelligent beings. For example, in Maths and Science, we weren't just told about ideas and how to apply them, but where they came from – how the fundamentals were derived. I remember being gobsmacked when in a maths lesson a teacher explained how calculus was derived by Newton and Leibniz. I was wowed by the world of ideas and inventions.

But I was also a lazy bugger. If something didn't interest me, I struggled to make the effort to do much work. French and Geography were at the bottom of the pile. In Geography, we seemed to spend an awful lot of time looking at maps! History was okay, although it was largely about English kings. English was great – apart from the grammar, and I spent many happy hours reading set books like To Kill A Mockingbird by Harper Lee and 1984 by George Orwell. I loved the Shakespeare plays that we did including Julius Caesar and Macbeth. We had readings in lessons, but unfortunately, none of the plays were ever performed at school. That would have been good.

The dreaded school uniform with short pants

I thought Maths was so so, and Music great but a waste of time as I wasn't learning an instrument[54], Religious Studies a joke, P.E. was OK apart from the cross country, and the sciences were fantastic. I enjoyed playing cricket and football but ruled myself out of any chance of being involved in school teams because I wouldn't turn up to school on a Saturday morning. The reason was it would have involved catching two buses and spending hours travelling there and back – my Dad didn't do taxi services. For the first few years at Hulme, I did well in English and Sciences and pretty well in everything else. I enjoyed Art, but with my Science bias, I was never going to be able to carry it as far as 'O' Level. Sculpture was my favourite, and I spent ages making a large black lobster-like creature out of a wire frame and plaster. When it was finished, it disappeared at the end of term and I didn't find out what happened to it until years later.

My first slip up was in maths. At the end of the fourth year, I got a poorish exam result and was summoned to see Fred Nerk. "How do you feel about maths – finding it hard lad?" " Er ..no.... not really" I replied, wondering what the implication of all this was. Well, the next year, I found out! I was dropped into a lower set with the 'dummies'. I spent the next two years up to 'O' level, rehashing trigonometry and logarithms that I could do with my eyes shut. If I'd realised the implications, I'd have fought and pleaded to be allowed to stay in a higher set – as it was, I still should have tried to get out, but I didn't. I suppose in the end, I wasn't interested enough in Maths to make the effort, and the lower set lessons were an easy gig. It still rankled though[55]. The irritating long-term outcome is that I have always felt slightly intimidated by maths, whereas if I'd been in a higher set, I would probably have done okay and would feel much more confident.

It was also not long before I fell foul of the archaic and arbitrary system of discipline which existed at Hulme for we not only had detentions but Saturday detentions! – and school prefects were allowed to

---

[54] This is my biggest regret. My parents couldn't really afford it at the time. I wished I'd pushed it and begged, borrowed or stolen one.

[55] There was one serious knock on effect though. Staying in that set had meant that I had missed out on learning more difficult maths as well as denting my confidence. This came back to haunt me when I got an 'O' level pass at Physics 'A' level – a failure I put down to my poor maths.

give lower school oiks like me detentions! Naturally enough, my first brush with this system was a complete farce. In the snowy winter of 68/69, we had slides and snowball fights galore, and in the general chaos and mayhem one break time, I was collared by a prefect for hitting him smack in the face with a snowball. Now, I know it wasn't me that did it – but in the time-honoured way of British summary justice, he'd managed to grab hold of the nearest likely suspect – and that was that – I was apprehended, tried, and sentenced in all of about 30 seconds.

I tried to believe it hadn't really happened to me whilst searching for the guilty rat who had no doubt departed snickering – but it was no use – next week, my name appeared on the dreaded list of those who were to spend Tuesday evening in detention. I was gutted, and for good reason – school finished at 3.45 pm, the school coach left at 4.00 pm, and detention ended at 4.30 pm – there was no way round it – I would have to endure the ball-ache of a trek home by dreaded public transport.

I say dreaded because I would have to walk at least a mile and then catch two buses to get home – this in itself would have been punishment enough for me – coming on top of 45 minutes of being kept in it was a disaster. There was also no way of hiding it from my parents. I would have to confess and cadge the bus fare. Did I get any sympathy from my parents?[56] Did they phone the school and complain? – or turn up and harangue the Headmaster? – no chance! Parents didn't do that in those days.

So I duly turned up at detention at the appointed hour. It was just my luck that 'Scruff' Parker – the immaculately dressed maths teacher – who had a devastating line in sarcasm – was taking the detention. Scruff was always feared and admired for his put downs. One of his favourites was "We have a wit here…….. a half wit!" I trudged in and sat down with the other miscreants. Scruff had a well-developed sense of superiority and read out the detention register with complete disdain as he surveyed the lowly rabble in front of him. I made the stupid mistake of sitting at the front. Then he noticed I was sitting at my desk without an exercise book "Thorp! – did you bring some work

---

[56] Naturally enough my mum was sympathetic - but if you got into trouble at school it was "Your own fault" and you'd just as likely get a bollocking from your parents to add to the bollocking from school. How times have changed!

with you!". I froze like a rabbit in the headlights of an oncoming juggernaut, and that was my undoing... "Nn no.. Sir" I stammered. "Well go home and come back next week with some work then!" Staggered, I had no choice but to leave the room looking like a complete plonker. As I left, I could feel the grins of my fellow detainees, most of whom were old hands, boring into my back. I looked at my watch; it was about 3.57 pm! – I legged it out of the building just as fast as I could only to find that the Alkrington coach had gone! So, in effect, I ended up with two detentions for the price of one.

Despite the fact that the whole affair was a pain in the ass, it was a valuable lesson for me – never again! – the next time it would be me sneaking off and snickering whilst some other poor sod took the blame – a lesson I put to good use in the remaining 6 years at Hulme. Of course, you can't always account for the unexpected – for example, I have only had one real good shiner in my life and that was given to me by a mate – Dave – one day when we were queuing up to go into a lesson. Some pillock behind us in the queue started pushing, and I went slam into Dave's back. He turned with amazing speed and socked me right in the eye! I was so gob-smacked as well as eye-smacked I was speechless. By the time I'd recovered my wits, we were in the lesson and it was too late for me to respond in any way.

Fights at school were fairly few and far between. When they happened, they immediately attracted a large and enthusiastic crowd. I had learned to fight in my last years at primary school, where I had a few bouts, but I soon discovered that discretion was the better part of valour in a school where most of the boys were bigger than me. My tongue was my best weapon, and I learned the happy knack of being able to take the piss with a subtlety that went over heads of most of the dickheads and bullies. I could also run pretty fast. After the detention debacle, I pretty soon perfected the technique of getting others to take the rap for the tricks that I got up to. Life at Hulme, as in general, was all about playing the system.

Of course, we had plenty of laughs, many of which were then firmly in the adolescent schoolboy milieu. In the lower school, I had the Deputy Head Cyril for French. Unfortunately, Cyril had a touch of the Finbar Saunders – he used to talk in double entendres. A friend, Marcus, and I used to sit at the back of his class almost crying with laughter, trying desperately to keep straight faces. We even used to write some of Cyril's best gems down and recount them to our mates, who were in other classes, at break time. The teachers always managed to provide us with plenty of amusement, especially when it was at the expense of fellow pupils.

The pettiness and piss taking of kids knows no bounds. Any weakness would be ruthlessly exploited. Some of the pupils came from the rural backwoods of Saddleworth, and one such was "Farmer". We used to mock him with "oo aar" Ambridge accents and say things like "Trousers down on the farm … with farmer" – this was guaranteed to provoke a furious response. A guy who had a large hooter was called "Nose" and suffered every pun on nose that we could devise. We even used to sing "I never promised you a nose garden" to wind him up. A friend of mine was so skinny he used to be known as 'Twiglet', and eventually, this was changed to 'Snapper' when some wit realised that he was so skinny you could probably easily snap his arms and legs. Fortunately, 'snapper' had the good sense to go with the flow rather than being enraged by his moniker.

At lunchtimes, we used to head down to the subterranean chamber, which was the refectory. There, we were served up all the timeless classics of school dinners; meat and two veg with soggy mashed potato in scoops, boiled-to-death carrots and sprouts, and all the favourite desserts; and spotted dick, sago, rice pudding, tapioca, chocolate sponge, apple crumble, and lumpy custard. Most of the time, we wolfed it down – we were growing lads. There was something eerily Dickensian about the whole scene. A crowd of scruffy ravenous boys in school uniform on benches at tables having food doled out of large tureens by busty matrons – a smelly fug of cabbage and sweaty boys – a cacophony of noise and bellowing prefects – one or two masters reluctantly slumming it with the herd.

After dinner, we raced out to the tennis courts up by the maths block to play football. The maths block was a collection of three prefab classrooms which I had always assumed were meant to be temporary but seemed to have been there for years. The tennis courts were tarmac, and although you could still see the lines, they hadn't been used for anything other than lunchtime football for years. The amazing thing about this small area was that we used to be able to have at least four different games of football going on simultaneously without interfering with each other[57] and with very few arguments. Football on the tennis courts was a serious business, always fast and furious, and was often played with a tennis ball if that was all we had access to. I usually played on the wing and scored lots of goals because I could shoot hard and accurately – as modelled on my hero at the time – Bobby Charlton. Steve Mingle and I used to play some great one twos around the defenders. He was a real slippery customer more like George Best, very difficult to tackle, and a good footballer.

A classic Hulme event occurred one lunchtime when Tastie[58] and I were helping the biology teacher Danny the 'Mallet' with the beehive that was in his biology lab. A large, angry bee flew out at us and landed on the lapel of Tastie's blazer. "Just leave it it's OK", said Mallet – but too late! Tastie instinctively took a swipe which brushed it off him and straight onto Mallet. I stood transfixed as the bee struck swiftly and stung Mallet right on the tip of his nose! Later that afternoon, we tried not crease up as Mallet taught our class with a huge red throbbing hooter!

Danny Mallet was one of the more popular teachers and had a reputation for being fair but hard. Not handing in homework on time meant an automatic detention and caused the class much amusement as we watched individuals trying and failing to get round him. I guess Mallet must have been somewhat accident-prone because he also set himself on fire in one of our lessons. I actually saw this happen, and it was one of those classic situations where you can see a disaster about to occur but in the second or so it takes are unable to get a warning out. He leaned on a desk with his back to a lit bunsen burner and set his shirt on fire!

That wasn't the only fun I had in the science labs. There were a bizarre collection of teachers in science – "Sammy" Bell, who was just completely bonkers; 'Doc Jock', a quietly spoken Scotsman, excellent teacher, nice bloke, and inveterate chain smoker who used to sneak into the room behind the chemistry lab for a crafty fag during lessons; 'Drooper', the biology teacher, Squadron Leader "Mary"

---

[57] That would include games being played at 90° to each other.
[58] My friend Tom Thorp. Tastie is pronounced as in pastie.

Moore; 'Abdul'; Danny 'Mallet'; and 'Iggy' Holt. Sammy Bell seemed to come from the Eddie Wearing school of Chemistry teaching and had some classic sayings which are reputed to include:

"I've taught you all I know, and you still know nothing";

"Watch the board while I run through it";

"I'm pointing this ruler now and, at the end of it, there is an idiot"; and

"Bring your mother in and I'll have it out in front of her",

all of which caused us to collapse laughing.

Where Mary Moore got his nickname from I don't know, but he was also fairly bonkers and quite deaf. I was once in a lesson when someone shouted out "Mary you cunt!", and he turned round and said "Yes I could!".

He used to make us do experiments with radioactive sources such as Thoron gas – the sort of stuff you wouldn't be allowed to take within a hundred miles of a school these days. How we survived I don't know. The highlight of Mary's lessons was a bizarre contraption he had. It consisted of a box with a dial on it that you plugged into the mains. Two cables came from the box with handles on the end. The idea was that you gripped the handles and someone turned the dial which increased the current flowing through the handles. Of course, at a certain current, your hands became clenched and you were unable to let go of the handles. This was ably demonstrated on one of the class, much to our amusement.

Most of the violence at school came from the teachers themselves. This was still the age of corporal punishment, and it was accepted that teachers could hit pupils and get away with it. If you had complained to your parents about being hit by a teacher, not only you would have not got much sympathy[59] but also you would have been regarded as a wimp by your peers. You took what was coming to you without complaining whether it was fair or not. That was how it worked in those days.

---

[59] After all they had it worse than we did when they were at school.

Apart from the official discipline – the cane – which was administered by the Deputy Head – unofficial sanctions included throwing chalks, or board dusters if you were unlucky, and 'cuffing' – a sharp blow to the back of the head. Fred 'Nerk', a maths teacher, had the canny knack of creeping up behind you while you were supposed to be working – but were in fact talking – and administering the said sharp blow to the back of the head whilst shouting "Cuff laddie!"[60]. In one lesson, he almost caught me out and I can still feel the draft of air as I ducked just in time and his hand passed about a millimetre from my head. He was also a dead shot with a board duster, and you had to learn to duck quickly there as well.

Only once in seven years at the school did I see an incident that was definitely over the top by the standards of the day – when an older teacher – who was a bit bonkers – struck a lad several times. Amazingly enough, he didn't retaliate – he could have flattened the teacher if he had wanted to.

When it was time to move into the fifth year, I made a classic cock up because my main interests were in English and Science and I was wishy washy about my fifth-year options in general. The end result was that I got shoved into a Latin set! I couldn't believe it! I could have had a nice cosy time in geography or history, but because of my choices and the timetable, I ended up with Latin! Bloody hell!!! Now, this was one I did try to get out of – but failed miserably because they were determined to rope in some victims – and so commenced two years of absolute torture. I somehow managed to pass Latin O level on the absolute minimum of work, and the end result now is that I know about as much Latin as the average person – that is, zip![61]

Another choice we had to make for the fifth year was what to do on Wednesday afternoon. Along with sport, there were various worthy

---

[60] I want to point out that I'm not complaining about any of this treatment. Of course it was wrong but that's how it was and parents, pupils and teachers all accepted the set up. I also wouldn't like anyone to have the impression that we were regularly beaten. Incidents of physical contact between teachers and pupils were reasonably uncommon.

[61] I still have my Latin textbook – the only one I ever kept from school. Such was the hatred with which I regarded Latin I was determined to take it and burn it! – but never did. For those who wish to know it is - ' Latin Course for Schools' Part II by L. A. Wilding M.A. published by Faber and Faber Ltd.

options like visiting old ladies and the Combined Cadet Force (CCF). Although I enjoyed sports and was reasonably good at football and cricket – actually, I was a good bowler but a lousy batsman until David Bottomley showed me how to improve my stance when I was about twelve – I was never quite good enough to get into the first team and couldn't be bothered to make the trip to school just to play in a lower team. In the end, I decided to opt for the CCF. Why? Wasn't it just about the antithesis of everything I stood for? – uniforms, hierarchy, mindless obedience, and violence! Yes, but it also had outdoor activities such as walking and orienteering, which I was very much into at the time, and linked together with the school's Adventure Training Group (ATG), which had outings several weekends a term where we would go to the Lakes, Peak District, and Snowdonia.

Thanks to the ATG, I have spent many happy hours in heavy cloud and driving rain on Black Hill, Bleaklow, and Kinder Scout. If it hadn't been for the fact that the ATG taught good map reading skills, I probably wouldn't be writing this now. Of course, I hated going to school in my RAF battledress and kit on a Wednesday, but it did have its compensations. For a start, some of the teachers were officers, had experienced WWII, and took the whole thing quite seriously – so you can see we are already getting into Captain Mainwaring territory and the potential for quite a lot of fun at their expense – in fact a typical CCF session what with parades and 'initiative exercises' would have provided Jimmy Perry and David Croft, the writers of Dad's Army, with plenty of material. It was a laugh – more quality piss taking. On one occasion, we were supposed to be on parade, on the tennis courts this was, and this real army twerp – Sergeant Major I think – tried to get us to actually stand properly to attention in ranks. We started laughing, and he went mad. The madder he got, the more we laughed. It was just like some sort of scene out of Dad's Army, my Dad's all-time favourite TV programme.

All of these bring me back to Latin because our teacher Ben Counsel[62] was an enthusiastic walker who frequently took part in ATG outings and enjoyed walking in places like the Lake District. During the absolute torture of forty-minute Latin lessons, it became my job to distract Ben by introducing mountain walking and ATG

---

[62] I am pleased to say I met Ben at a school reunion in 2015 - see below.

discussion into the lesson – this was pretty well guaranteed to send Ben off into a ten-minute reverie and monologue about recent and forthcoming ATG expeditions – thus was vital relief gained for the class. Of course, it always put me under pressure as the clock ticked by and classmates gave me looks of "Come on! – get him talking" but also gave me something never to be taken lightly at school – kudos.

One of the most memorable and exciting ATG outings of that time happened at Easter 1973. A coach load set off for the Lake District to do a traverse of Fairfield, the plan being to cross from east to west. Fairfield is 2863 feet high and lies at the centre of a group of fells between Patterdale and Grasmere. Thus, we arrived at Patterdale on the Sunday Morning in fine but cold weather with snow on the tops and clouds threatening more to come. We split into two groups and ascended by St Sunday Crag and Dove Crag. I was in the group that went via St Sunday Crag, and a very good walk it was too with spectacular views of Ullswater and Helvellyn. I had a bit of bad luck on the summit of St Sunday Crag at 2756 feet when I stopped to take a photo and one of my gloves was blown away in a gust of wind. As we left and descended towards Deepdale Hause, the pass between St Sunday Crag and Fairfield, the wind began to strengthen. At the Hause, we were faced with an ascent of about 800 feet over Cofa Pike to Fairfield. It was a fabulous sight. Dazzling sunshine and the narrow snow encrusted ridge rising to Cofa Pike with the Summit above in cloud.

As we ascended, we were battling against the wind but came across sheltered ground higher up. By the time we had climbed over the summit of Cofa Pike, about 200 ft from the top, we were in thick cloud with poor visibility. But the big shock was arriving on the summit plateau to be hit by a wall of wind and driving snow. It was a white-out; it was impossible to see more than a yard in front of your face and almost impossible to stand upright. The volume of driving snow coming at us was almost suffocating. By bending into the wind, we were able to make slow progress forwards —but where was forwards? We were now dependent on compass for route finding – we had to get off the summit as soon as possible – and there were serious crags to the north. We had to shout to each other to make ourselves heard

as we fumbled to check the map and compass huddled together......
which went something like this:

"We've 'ad it Sir!, we've 'ad it[63]
H----, this is desperate!
I can't look round. I can't see anything. Wind and hail's too hard to face into.
What do we do next then?
Shouldn't we get out of this?
I wonder where the others are?
I'll have to get my mitts on.
I'll have to put my hands in my bag to try to warm them.
Where are my mitts? Can you see my mitts in there, Darryl?
Get my mitts on! Get my mitts on! Thanks!
We shouldn't have split up like that you know!
Sorry about that P----, but when I looked round, you were all quite close.
What do we do next then?
We can't stay here.
These hailstones are like little bits of glass being fired at you face all the time.
Right, let's get out of this, where's south?
Who has a compass handy?
Let's have a look at that map, I can't see a thing!
There's ice all over your glasses and your hair.
I'll take them off then. Good! South! Where's South?
South's over that way Sir!
Right, that way then! let's get out of this!"

By linking arms together, we were able to head south – the safest way off the summit in low visibility, and the direction of the ridge to Ambleside. It was a huge relief to get off the summit, and by the time we had descended a few hundred feet, we were out of the snow and the wind had dropped. We sat gratefully in a sheltered part of the Great Rigg ridge to eat our sandwiches before the descent to Grasmere. It was a great day out on the hills and one I'll never forget.

---

[63] This is part of Ben Counsel's written account of the white-out on Fairfield which he wrote shortly after the event and distributed to the participants.

Of course, whilst in the CCF, I got up to a number of escapades, one of which involved me getting my First Class marksman's badge. I'd found difficulty shooting with a .22 rifle right-handed because I've never been able to close my left eye on its own. So, after a poor start, I began to shoot left-handed and soon improved. On the fateful day of my marksman's badge, half a dozen of us were in the school 25 yard shooting range. We took our shots at the targets, and then I was told to go and fetch them. In the split second in which I took my neighbour's target down, I saw he had a really good grouping – so I switched targets. Naturally enough, nobody noticed and the afternoon ended with one very disappointed cadet muttering "I could've sworn I did better than that" – but targets can't lie, can they? – and I was now a marksman first class!

One of the things that I really hated doing on sports afternoons was the dreaded cross-country run to which we were subjected lower down the school. Of course, there was no country as such to run through, but that didn't stop the sadistic PE teachers from making us do it. Except when being chased by bullies or irate husbands,[64] I've never been any good at running. I used to make a token effort, walking most of the way, and generally coming in late, just ahead of the real weeds.

By the 6th Form, I'd decided that my favourite subject was Biology, and that I wanted to be a scientist. The school had also helped me develop strong socialist tendencies. My awakening had begun at about 14, when I became aware that the school had a caste, or class, system which mirrored that of the outside world. All the school below the 6th Form were the plebs – the great unwashed. By the time you reached the 6th Form, you were comfortable middle class, and if you had aspirations to upper middle class, you became a prefect. Teachers were the ruling class, with one or two Dukes and Barons thrown in and, naturally, Sidney was King. Only God was above the Headmaster. Hulme Grammar School made me a socialist, and nothing has changed since.

---

[64] This is a slight exaggeration. I have been chased by girlfriend's fathers and boyfriends of girls I got too friendly with.

The weird thing about all this was that no one that I knew of seemed bothered about it or aware of the glaring inequalities and social injustice of it all – apart from me. They either just accepted it and went along with it or accepted it and tried to play the system, and climb the greasy pole. I can't recall anyone ever wanting to overthrow the system – bar me. I also can't recall any pupils mentioning a word of politics, even pinkish Labour politics the whole time I was there. Of course, there were rebels, but they were more interested in music and girls than anything else. There were however one or two rather more enlightened 'lefty' teachers who I got to know in the sixth form[65].

At first, I was baffled, but then I realised it was not wholly surprising because most of the pupils were the scion of the well-off middle classes – although there was a fair-sized minority of lower-middle-class and working-class kids. If anything, my experience there made me realise how powerful and difficult to break down hierarchies are. But it got worse. Two of my friends, Tastie and Marcus, had started 'helping out' at parent evenings and the like. For me, this was beyond comprehension. Why would anyone be daft enough to return to school in the evening voluntarily? The answer soon became clear as both were named as prefects for the following year in the Upper 6th.

In the Upper 6th, about a dozen of us or so were rebels and we were tolerated and marginalised rather than repressed. We were only ones who weren't prefects. The British ruling class have always been experts at dealing with dissent, and Hulme was no exception. But anyway, the rebellion was more about style than substance. What passed for rebellion at Hulme in those days? – well, we refused to get our hair cut and wore coloured shirts – officially, you could only wear white or grey shirts; and we listened to bands like Pink Floyd, Genesis,

---

[65] Sidney (the Head) made an impassioned speech in assembly for us to encourage our parents to vote Tory in the 1970 general election in order to preserve the school. It would have seemed quite natural for people to express Tory views in such an environment. After all, most parent of pupils were either professionals, business owners or the 'aspiring' lower middle class. There were probably a few Labour voting teachers but otherwise socialist views would probably have been seen as subversive.

In my CCF uniform at Warwick Road. Look how happy I am to be wearing it. Note the haircut

Captain Beefheart, Todd Rundgren, and Soft Machine; smoked[66]; and generally treated the place with contempt. But we attended nearly all our lessons and did nearly all our work – the boat hardly rocked! Most of us hated the place simply because it was so square. We used to hang around in the non-prefects 6th Form common room into which girls from Hulme's Girls Grammar were allowed[67] and, as a rule, didn't mix with the prefects at all. I can remember a prefect coming into our common room one lunchtime and telling us to stop gambling – we were playing three card brag for money – only to be told to "fuck off" or he would "get his head kicked in". He never returned. But then

---

[66] I started in April 1975 not long before 'A' levels – see next chapter. Smoking, of course was not allowed, though I can recall prefects smoking in their common room when I was lower down the school – no doubt the rule didn't apply to them.
[67] Hulme Grammar School for Girls was on the same site in an adjoining building but it might as well have been 100 miles away for all the contact we had with them. I can remember playing cards in the common room and Hulme girls being there. For sure not many of the girls apart from one or two of the more adventurous ones mixed with us.

where would you rather have been – stuck in a room with a load of conformist prefect twerps – or playing cards with the girls from Hulme Grammar?

Indirectly, this resulted in my one and only direct brush with Sidney the Head. He had a canny knack of coming out of his office, which was near the main entrance[68], and grabbing passers by whom he thought were skiving or misbehaving in some other way – it was suspected that he must have had some sort of spy camera. One day, he dived out, caught me, and dragged me into his office. Imagine my amazement when I saw my missing big black lobster on cabinet behind his desk! He proceeded to harangue me about my long hair and purple shirt, and the exchange went something like this – "I know you come from a good family… why are you behaving like this". 'What the fuck do you know about my family' I thought, 'I'm not one of your creepy prefects'. "Have you anything to say for yourself", he said. "No Sir" I said. "Then GET OUT!", he shouted, and I found myself back in the corridor. In the heat of the moment, I forgot to ask for my lobster back. I wonder if it is still there?

Sidney even had an arrangement with the local barber. I kid you not. Pupils with 'long' hair were sent to this demon barber to have a haircut. Most entered expecting to have a trim, but all came back scalped. You could always tell when someone had been sent there. The demon barber was on Sidney's payroll. Maybe he was an ex-teacher or pupil?

I had a run-in with Abdul when we were close to taking A levels. One day when Doc Jock was off sick, we had Abdul for chemistry instead. He wasn't teaching A levels and thus had a big chip on his shoulder, and we looked down our noses at him because of it. By this stage in his career, he had become more fastidious than ever and had developed a set of petty and officious rules for his lab. We arrived early that period and sauntered into the room[39]. I looked around and couldn't believe my luck. On a large blackboard on a side wall, Abdul had written an absurd set of rules in capital letters using a red chalk. It read like this:

---

[68] The front door was only for use by teachers, parents, visitors and sixth formers. The rest used to have to use a side entrance.
[69] Upper sixth formers didn't deign to wait outside a classroom.

16 SMALL STOOLS MUST BE KEPT AT THE FRONT TWO BENCHES AND 20 LARGE STOOLS MUST BE KEPT AT THE REAR TWO BENCHES

This was asking for it. With two simple strokes of a board duster, I removed two "S"s from these instructions so that "STOOLS" became "TOOLS" and sat down, well satisfied with such a straightforward but devastating opportunity, and began to savour the fun. By this time, the room had filled up and there were one or two schoolboy sniggers. Then Abdul came in, and it went quiet. He began by giving us a stern lecture on how we should not have entered the lab before he arrived. This would have been funny enough, but by now, the word had gone round and the room was beginning to fill with suppressed laughter.

Realising that mirth was rising around him but still unaware of the true cause, Abdul went into a rant about how as sixth formers we should be more responsible. That was too much for some and was greeted with open laughter. I watched Abdul closely. He was getting madder and madder, sensing he was the butt of a joke but unable to tell what it was. Then I saw him following the eyes of one or two of the laughers towards the blackboard, and at last, the penny dropped! The long anticipated explosion occurred! "Who did this!" he screamed, blazing with anger. Nobody spoke, and for a couple of seconds, it went quiet .... Then the silence was then suddenly broken by the sound of uncontrollable laughter, closely followed by more rage from Abdul.

Of course, it was a stand-off. The first rule of the schoolboy is 'honour amongst thieves' – you don't grass up your fellow pupils. Alas! There never was much honour amongst our thieves and with Abdul threatening to keep us there 'til he found out who'd done it – it was the last period of the day – it was inevitable that after about 10 minutes some pimply pillock would grass me up. I wasn't the only one to be punished with a detention; my mates Barry and Steve were also roped in for pretty much non-stop laughter through the whole of Abdul's threats and feet stamping. Steve was laughing so much he fell off his 'tool'. I wasn't worried; even if I had had a detention, it would have been worth every second, but I knew it would never happen. We were only weeks away from taking A levels and therefore pretty much untouchable – certainly by the likes of Abdul, and in reality, he knew it.

Even that wasn't quite the low point of my Hulme school career however. Though there were only a few days left, I, and most of my mates, were to sink even lower. On the last day of school, we went to the pub at lunch time. I had never done this before. I can't recall the name of the pub, but it wasn't far from the school, probably on Ashton Road. There must have been at least 30 or so of us there and some sixth formers from the Girls school as well, and naturally enough, we all got drunk. And so we staggered back to school for the final afternoon, and the send off, in the school hall. This was provided by an 'important' old boy. He was a bluff, Colonel Blimpish sort of chap who proceeded to lecture us about the importance of becoming an Old Boy and some stuff about our future careers or something.

Within several minutes of him starting, people were beginning to get bored and restless and there was a certain amount of burping and farting going on. This then progressed into whispering and a gradually increasing hum of chatter. Then from the back of the room, there were some muffled cries of "Ger off!" Last day, and pissed or not, my Hulme 'antenna' was still working at full power and I looked round to see a purple-faced Sidney lurking at the back of the hall. He lurched forwards and ran onto the platform and screamed at us that we were a disgrace and that we should all go home. So er.... that was it. My time at Hulme was over. I can remember feeling great – escape at last!

So what did I get out of Hulme Grammar School for Boys? A good education? In some respects yes. Academically, the school was fairly good, but then the pupils were mostly fairly bright, middle class, and well motivated. The teaching was mixed but reasonably rigorous, which I liked. I hated the stuffiness, snobbery, and class-ridden pretensions of the place. I also hated the fact that it was single sex. But would I have done as well academically if I had been to the local comp with my friends from Warwick Road? 'I'm not sure – as it was, I cocked up my 'A' levels anyway – but I don t blame Hulme for that. Girls would certainly have been a great distraction from work. As it was, I spent some of my time there in a haze of sexual fantasies derived from the copies of Penthouse and Mayfair that were passed around the place in lessons. On the whole, I had a good time, but I was relieved to see the back of the place when I left, and couldn't wait to get to university. I don't regret being there, and I don't hold any grudges. Maybe, one day, I'll even want to go back and have a look at the place.

Well, in fact, I did go back. I was invited to a fortieth reunion by one of my old schoolmates. This was held at the Marriott hotel near Manchester Airport, which made it easier for old boys and girls who had moved away to get there. Guess what? My decision to go was driven to a large extent by curiosity about who would attend and how they had changed and fared over the years. Remarkably, the event was attended by one of my old teachers, Ben Counsel, who was in his 80s. I really enjoyed it, and the following year, I attended the annual school dinner. Again, this was driven largely by curiosity to see the old place again. Will I ever return? If I make it to the 50th, I just might.

That's me with the milk bottle. Tastie is on my right

Chapter 9
TEENAGE ANGST

When I was 10 years old, I came of age in two important ways. Firstly, I stopped believing in God, and secondly, I had my first erection. I hasten to add that the two were not connected! – but they did come at about the same time. The second event, looking back, was slightly comical because I was so completely innocent that I had no idea it was going to happen. For a brief time, I was tempted to tell my parents, but something held me back. I knew instinctively that what was happening wasn't a bad thing, and not the sort of thing you told your Mum and Dad about. It felt good. Not having an older brother, I had to make investigations with the help of friends who had, and over the next couple of months or so, I pieced the whole thing together. So that's what it was all about – sex! I guess I had had some twinges down there for a couple of years beforehand and I was beginning to develop an interest in girls – and this accelerated rapidly afterwards. By the time I left junior school, I had had three 'girlfriends' – Jane, Yvonne, and Margaret. Maggie lived on Mainway, which was one of the posher parts of Alkrington. You can tell it was true love because one day, I went round to see her in the pouring rain. Her mother regarded me as a scally from the less desirable part of Alkrington and wouldn't let me in the house, and we ended up sitting in her back garden for an hour or so holding hands.

My parents never talked to me about sex as such, but they did provide me with some sex education. They got hold of a pamphlet from the Doctor's[70], and my Dad told me I needed to read it. I took it to bed one night and pored over it. My recollection is that there were no photos or pictures of naked people or the 'act' but the usual anatomical drawings of the workings of male and female private parts along with words like: the man inserts his penis into the woman's

---

[70] Big shout out to my doctor here. He was Doctor Leveson, an old school guy who used to check your pulse and take your temperature. I always felt comfortable with him and he helped me when I was older and going through a period of depression. A great bloke.

vagina – so that's how it works! What was amusing about all this was that when I woke up in the morning, the pamphlet had disappeared! Nothing more was said, but my Dad did give me a porno mag a couple of years later. Before you recoil in horror, it was typical for men, including married men, to have porno mags in those days. That's just how it was.

But what about God? Well, I had gone along with all the God stuff at school, sung hymns, and soaked up most of what I'd been told. My parents weren't religious, so I had no pressure to conform to any religious beliefs and I hadn't even been christened. So, one day, I had my Nietzsche moment – God was dead. Why didn't I believe? All the stuff I was told did nothing for me. The Bible just wasn't credible to me and clearly belonged in a bygone age. Jesus sounded like a very good bloke, but that was about all.....a very good bloke, someone to look up to and respect but not a supernatural being – plus the establishment were pushing it all at us to make us conform – so it couldn't possibly be right, could it?

I also had a natural suspicion about religious people which I've never lost. Why were they so keen for me to believe? What business was it of theirs if I didn't, and why were they trying to impose their rules on me? Ceasing to believe in God was liberating – and anyway, who could like a god that was omnipotent but imposed such senseless and needless suffering on people. What on earth was the point of Heaven and who would want to go there? It could only be full of nauseatingly self-righteous people. Imagine spending eternity surrounded by Christians!

Of course, not believing in God is good for you. Why? Because if you've got any sense of natural curiosity and an enquiring mind, you have to start to try and figure things out for yourself – and that's exactly what I began to do next. I decided that if there was no God, then it was down to people to sort out the world's problems without any help from above, and it was up to us to find out what the universe was all about. Thus, I became interested in politics, philosophy, and science. Having read and admired George Orwell's books and been made acutely aware of the class system and non-sensical hierarchy system at school, it seemed perfectly logical to me to become a socialist, or even better still an anarchist! Anarchism by George

Woodcock was the book I came across which made me question the whole system we lived under.

But I'm getting a little ahead of myself. I was soon to leave Alkrington County Primary for Hulme Grammar School. At the time, I didn't want to go. Most of my friends were going to the local comprehensive. But I also realised that because half of them were Catholic, that I would not be going with them anyway. The first year at Hulme was really difficult. A gap had opened up between me and the kids in my street. We no longer had as much in common. They had new friends that I didn't know. The saving grace of Hulme was that some of my contemporaries from junior school went with me. In the first few years at Hulme, I used to meet up with the Bottomley Brothers (known affectionately as the Bumly brothers), Martin Kaye, Robin Brown, Simon Croydon, Alick Cross, and others, but most of my friends lived on the other side of Alkrington – the older, posher bit. We used to play cricket a lot, especially in the summer holidays, and I used to cycle all over Alkrington to meet up with my mates. It still wasn't quite the same as having friends on your doorstep though, and in the long winters, when it was dark at four o'clock, I was pretty well stuck on my own a lot of the time.

The years from eleven to sixteen were pretty grim socially in the winter. I was stuck indoors during the week. We didn't have a landline until I was thirteen – so if I wanted to call anyone, I had to walk up to the local shops. Most of my local mates from Hulme seemed to be locked up doing homework in the evenings, and my other school friends lived too far away for it to be feasible to visit them.

While I am talking about going to the phonebox, I ought to mention one of the most unusual experiences of my life. I'd gone up to Alkrington shops to make a phone call – this was the days of push button A and button B – and after I came out of the phonebox and walked towards the shops. Looking up, I saw a bright light in the sky. It was cigar-shaped, with no wings, so it couldn't be a plane. It moved slowly away across the sky. Had I seen a UFO? I looked round, but there was no one about. I wanted to jump up and down and shout "look at that", but it was pointless. I watched the object move slowly across the sky until it disappeared behind buildings and then trudged home. I was amazed and transfixed. What was I going to tell my parents? I got home and went into the lounge where my Dad was in the armchair as usual watching the local news on the BBC – Look Northwest. After a couple of minutes, I was amazed to see a report that hundreds of people had phoned in and reported seeing a UFO over Manchester! So I wasn't alone. It was definitely a UFO, but whether it was filled with aliens I have no idea.

So what did I do with my time? Well, apart from certain activities which can allegedly cause blindness, I was able to indulge my passion for reading. Hulme was fairly good on encouraging reading and introducing us the classics that I wasn't aware of such as To Kill a Mockingbird by Harper Lee and Animal Farm by George Orwell. I absolutely devoured books. I could read a 200-odd-page book in a few hours. My preference was very much for what would now be called 20th-century classics, but many of these were too new to be regarded as classics in those days. These included books by writers such as Graham Greene, George Orwell, H G Wells, John Wyndam, Jean Paul Sartre, Albert Camus, John Steinbeck, Franz Kafka, and C S Forester's Hornblower series. I also loved all the Sherlock Holmes books by Arthur Conan Doyle, and, after reading the Hobbit, when I was eight, I went on to read and enjoy Lord of the Rings many times.

Apart from reading, I spent a lot of time listening to music – mainly classical music – favourites included my first EP, the Karelia Suite by Sibelius, the 1812 Overture by Tchaikovsky, the Firebird Suite by Stravinsky, and my bestie the Enigma variations by Elgar. I was never a big Beethoven fan, and I preferred 20th century classical music. As I have already mentioned, I loved bands like the Beatles, Rolling Stones, Kinks, Traffic, Jethro Tull, Van Der Graaf Generator, and Pink Floyd, but the first rock album I bought was Benefit by Jethro Tull when I was 12.

One of my friends who made the transition from Alkrington to Hulme was Simon. We had a few adventures together. He lived in the leafy part of Alkrington near Alkrington Hall. When I was fourteen, we went on holiday to Anglesey. His parents took us there and back, and after we'd arrived, they pretty much left us to our own devices. In fact, I can't remember seeing them for the long weekend we were there. He brought along a mate whose name I can't remember, and the three of us slept in a tent in a field which had a couple of horses in it.

Teenage Angst

We had a number of adventures while we were there, which included me winning a few quid on a slot machine in a local cafe. I was on a winning streak, and a few quid was a lot of money to me in those days. We found a local stream which we followed and by pure luck managed to catch an Eel that was in it; this involved getting fairly wet – Simon fell on it! We took the Eel back to camp and managed to cook it, but when it came to the crunch, I decided I didn't fancy it. I also had my first ever cigarette, given to me by Simon's pal, but it made me feel sick and I didn't finish it. Thankfully, it put me off fags for a few years. Of course, none of us could really cook, and I think we survived mainly on tea, cornflakes, burgers from the cafe, and Mars bars.

The highlight of the holiday happened in the middle of one night when one of the horses, which was running round the field for some reason, managed to get tangled in the guy ropes of our tent and ripped the side off! Being rudely awakened was quite a shock, but there was little we could do in the dark! We managed to 'fix' the canvas tent by sewing it up, and fortunately, it didn't rain for the rest of our stay.

I had another fishing adventure with Simon and a couple of friends at one of the lodges near Alkrington Hall. We had a net, and I'm not sure how we managed it, but we caught a Pike. It was a large, very feisty creature. But we succeeded in subduing it between us. The Eel and the Pike were the only successes I've ever had when fishing.

Simon had an older brother and sister who used to have wild parties when their parents were away. I remember going to one of these parties when I was fifteen in the hope of finding a girlfriend, but given that most of the party-goers were over eighteen, I didn't really stand a chance. At least I managed to have a few beers and a sneaky couple of puffs on a joint.

The other notable incident in my escapades with Simon occurred one Sunday afternoon when I visited his house and we went out in the back garden where his Dad was digging. "Where are you going?" said his Dad, "have you finished your homework?" "Fuck that!" said Simon, at which has Dad became enraged and, spade in hand, lunged towards us, shouting and swearing We both turned and legged it, managing to jump over the fence as he chased us wielding the spade! Good job it was a rickety old fence

By the sixth form at Hulme, I'd lost touch with Simon and had a new group of friends, and several years after leaving Hulme, I was shocked and saddened to hear that he had committed suicide[71].

So, I kept on reading, listening to music, and going out to meet my local friends from Hulme as often as I could. I was desperate for a girlfriend, but the opportunities were limited. I went to the local youth club a couple of times, but this wasn't a great success because I didn't know anyone there. Most of the kids were at the local comps and in groups. I was an outsider.

As I got older and could go further afield, things improved. I'd already started going into Manchester on a Saturday, having a look round and visiting my cherished place at the time, Sherratt and Hughes bookstore in St Annes Square, where I spent hours browsing through books.

When I was fifteen, in January 1973, I had my first pint in a pub. It was just before my sixteenth birthday. I'd started going to a youth club in Victoria Avenue, Blackley, and the pub was nearby. So, I plucked up courage and entered a pub for the first time in my life! It was gloomy, busy, and smoke-filled, and there was a queue at the bar. I think this gave me an advantage, but I can't be sure. Although I was obviously young-looking, I'd managed to cultivate a pair of sideburns which were trendy at the time and made me look older. Fortunately for me, I'd checked the contents of my pocket before asking for a drink. I only had fourteen pence! Beer was sixteen pence a pint! Just as I was reeling from this, the barman asked me what I wanted. Somehow, I managed to maintain my composure, and trying to look nonchalant noticed, they had mild on tap – "Pint of mild please". Mild was fourteen pence a pint! So I got away with it! Retiring to a gloomy corner, I gulped down the beer and left as quickly as possible.

I'm not quite sure how, but I continued to get away with underage drinking until after I'd reached my eighteenth birthday. I remember going to the Tandle Hill Tavern with my best mate Dave (of whom more later) about 6 months before my eighteenth and buying a round. When it was his turn, he went to the bar and he was asked his age! He was a couple of years older than me and over twenty! He came back muttering and cursing as if it was my fault!

---

[71] I was told this by an acquaintance. I'd hope he was still with us.

Of course, pubs were very different in those days. Most people smoked, and there were many pubs with brown nicotine-stained walls, and reeked of fags, as well as punters with yellow nicotine-stained fingers. Many had a bar and a lounge. Very few women went into pubs on their own, and if they went in, they went with their husbands and boyfriends and stayed in the lounge – where beer was usually a couple of pence more expensive. Occasionally, you would see a couple of older women drinking together. It wasn't the done thing for women to drink pints either. They would usually drink halves or a glass of wine, or a Babycham.

So the bar or tap was the noisy den where the men hung out and smoked, joked, laughed, and argued – and played darts and pool, both of which I enjoyed. As for the beer on offer, it wasn't great, not by today's standards. Of course, there were some very good bitters around, such as Bass, Double Diamond, and Tetleys, but much depended on how well they were kept by the landlord. There were also some pretty awful stuff as well. Warneys always springs to mind when I think back – the infamous Warneys Red in particular, which was pretty gruesome stuff! I tried it once and nearly spat out the first mouthful! I had to drink it though. I couldn't afford to waste a pint.

Many pubs were tied to breweries and only served their bitter, mild, and Guinness, which was pretty ubiquitous at that time. One of the key differences was the lack of varieties on offer. In those days, very few people drank lager. That all changed after the long hot summer of 1976 when people (men actually) discovered a taste for lager, largely because it was chilled. Carlsberg – not particularly well kept or tasty Carlsberg – became the drink of choice for many, and it stuck.

Some pubs had juke boxes, which were great, and contained real 45 singles, and 'fruit machines' which you could gamble on, but that was about it. I never saw any live music in a pub when I was a teenager, but then I did most of my drinking in Middleton, Oldham, and occasionally Rochdale, with my mate Dave who lived there.

While I'm writing about booze and pubs, I have to make special mention of The Old Boars Head in Middleton and The City Arms in Manchester. The Old Boars was, and still is, a great pub. In the 1970s, if you went in there on a Saturday night, they had guys waiting on who used to wear white Tetleys jackets and bring the beer to your table. The beer was always excellent. Coincidentally, The City Arms was a Tetleys pub. In those days, the front room was the lounge and the back room the bar. It was run by a lovely old couple. Those who used the bar got served through a hatch at the back of the lounge bar – another great pint of Tetleys! I still visit whenever I'm in Manchester, and I have to say it's still a great pub – recommended.

Me and my Dad near Blackstone Edge

Nowadays, we take craft ales for granted. Much of the improvement in the variety and quality of British beer started in the 1970s with the Campaign for Real Ale, better known as CAMRA. My Dad was a keen member, and we always used to seek out the best beers we could find when we were on holiday.

Teenage Angst

One of my favourite activities outside of reading and listening to music was fell walking. I had already been on plenty of walks with my Dad and devoured all of Wainwrights guides by the time I'd become a teenager. I went mainly to the Pennine moors around Manchester, and the Lake District, which I loved with a passion, and still do – the lake water glistening in the sunlight, the breeze on the leaves in the forest, autumn colours, and the blue sky behind the dark ridges of the fells. My heroes were the great British climbers of the times – Chris Bonnington, Douglas Easton, and Don Whillans – also known as "The Villain". But who to walk with? I did some walks with my Dad, but none of my best chums at school were interested.

The lads in Hulme Gully on Tryfan

The last great walking adventure I had with my Dad was on an Easter weekend in North Wales; we went with two of my school friends, Tom Thorp (Tastie) and Dave Whitehead. We stayed in the youth hostel in the Idwal valley and climbed Tryfan on the first day and then Snowdon via Crib Gogh. The weather was fantastic on the day we climbed Tryfan. Snowdon was not quite so good as you can see from the photo, but it didn't rain. While I was clinging onto rocks on Crib Gogh, an old guy appeared walking nonchalantly along the crest. I said "You must have a head for heights!", at which he replied "I'm seventy I'm too old to be afraid of dying".

I subscribed to the Youth Hostel Association's newsletter which had a personal ads section for walkers, and so I put in an ad to try and meet people of my own age locally. Through the ad, I met Sylvia, Dave, and Denise. Denise and Sylvia lived locally – although Sylvia was in Langley, which was a bit of trek from our house, but you could get a bus – and Dave lived in Castleton near Rochdale. We became good friends, and Dave Fletcher became my best friend.

Dave and I had a number of escapades on the fells. We did plenty of walking and climbing in the peak district at places like Windgather rocks and Summit Quarry. I remember us both abseiling off the top of Summit Quarry in the old-fashioned way using only a rope. You wouldn't catch me doing that these days! I can't say I was a particularly great climber, and I was happy to let Dave take the lead. We also did plenty of walking on the moors of Kinder Scout, Bleaklow, and Black Hill.

But it was the lakes and North Wales that we loved best. We had a great camping weekend in which we walked up to Sprinkling Tarn and stayed by the tarn for two nights. There's nothing like rising early with the Sun and crawling out of your tent to be surrounded by mountains on a beautiful morning. We walked over Great End, up to Scafell Pike and Scafell. The weather was superb, and at one point, we were above the clouds. On both nights, we walked down the Sty Head Pass to the Wasdale Head Inn and got pissed in the bar. The trek back up to the tent was a bit of dodgy ordeal – just one torch and no head torches – but we survived. We also stayed in Ennerdale and did Pillar and Great Gable, two of my favourite mountains.

Our dodgiest trip was in winter with snow and ice. We went on a coach from Manchester with a walking club, and when we arrived in Glenridding, we set off on our own to climb Helvellyn. The Helvellyn range was covered in snow, and the conditions were great.

We had ice axes and a rope but no crampons. I'm not sure we knew what we were letting ourselves in for, and, as we approached Striding Edge, it became clear that it was covered in snow and ice. We had to make a decision. Striding Edge looked dodgy without crampons, but we decided to press ahead. We roped up and walked along the crest of the Edge because it seemed the safest option. The funny thing was although we were very exposed with a drop of hundreds of feet on either side, I don't recall being scared. I guess I was too focused on survival. We even joked that if one of us fell, the best bet was for the other to go over there opposite side!

We made it safely to the coll below Helvellyn and met a Park Ranger who was descending, and we stopped for a chat before the last climb up to the summit. On top, the weather was perfect and you could see for miles. We were surrounded by snowy peaks. That was the best day on the fells I've ever had. I only wish I had some photos to share.

L-R: Tastie, Me and Dave on Crib Goch

We also had a trip in snow to North Wales to the Idwal valley. It was Easter 1974. We met at Chorlton Street bus station to catch the coach, and I noticed that Dave had an ice axe on his rucksack. "What's that for?" I said. "Haven't you listened to the weather forecast", he said, "there's snow and ice in North Wales!". I hadn't and I didn't have my ice axe. Once again, we had glorious weather and we climbed Glyder Fach and Glyder Fawr on the first day. The ascent of Glyder Fach from the youth hostel was via Llyn Bochlwyd. Fatefully, we decided to go straight up the mountain from there. Dave led the way, making steps, and fortunately, the snow was of very good quality. After a couple of 100 feet, I looked down and I didn't like what I saw. If I fell from here, I could be in real trouble. "Look Dave I'm going down", I said, "I'll take the easy route and meet you on the summit". He agreed. Now began a nerve racking, slow, careful journey down where I descended step by step using the footholds as handholds. I got to the bottom safely. Phew!

I was wearing very thick mittens, but my hands were frozen by the time I reached the bottom. I set off and without any real difficulties climbed to the summit by the easier route, where I was very pleased to see Dave in one piece. We had survived another scrape! The outcome was later that evening, when we returned to the Youth Hostel, my hands were sore, and covered in blisters, not quite frostbite but painful enough. Anyway, I survived! The next day, we climbed Y Garn and had a glorious day, one of the best I have ever had in the mountains.

Dave and I spent plenty of time in pubs and had trips to Manchester where we visited pubs such as the aforementioned favourite, the City Arms, and went to gigs. We were both fans of Santana, and when I occasionally went over to Dave's house, he'd always put a Santana album on while we were planning our next adventures and drinking Newcastle Brown from the local offy. The album was usually Abraxas, or my favourite Caravanserai.

One of the best gigs I've ever been to was the Mahavishnu Orchestra at the Free Trade Hall in Manchester in January 1975. It was a perfect treat for my 18th birthday. When Dave and I arrived in the foyer, we were amused to see a dressed-up couple, he wearing a tux and she in an expensive frock. They must have thought it was a classical concert surely? Or maybe that was how they always dressed for gigs? I don't remember seeing them inside the hall though. This was the gig where they played their album Visions of The Emerald Beyond. What a gig! – mind-blowing guitar from John McLaughlin and Jean Luc Ponty's sublime violin playing. I still have the vinyl I purchased at the time.

Another great gig was Jethro Tull at the Opera house in Manchester. It was the Warchild tour in 1974, and they opened with Thick as a Brick. As soon as I heard about the gig through New Musical Express,

I jumped on a bus and went down there to buy tickets. I was the first person there and had my pick of tickets. I noticed that there was a box overlooking the stage which would be perfect. It was expensive, ten quid!, but there would be four of us there. I went with Dave, Sylvia, and Denise. The great view of the stage was a luxury. I was absolutely enchanted; they were still my number one band at the time.

My copy of Visions of the Emerald Beyond

Dave and I managed to gatecrash some parties and went to a cracking Party in Sale. We got there by bus. Many beers were drunk, and the party went on very late. So late, the booze was running out. We even ended up drinking Martinis from the bottle we were that desperate. Needless to say, we were both pissed and I then managed to trap off with an attractive young lady who was about the same age as me. We sneaked upstairs to an unoccupied bedroom. Some kissing and fumbling went on, but not much more; I was absolutely legless. We ended up holding hands, sitting on the front doorstep as the Sun came up. I gave her my address and never expected anything from her, but a few days later, I received a passionate letter. I wanted to reply, but my focus was on university, now not so far away, so I didn't. I've always regretted not replying to her.

With Sylvia and Denise, we set up a local group called Middleton Mountain Club (MMC). We advertised locally and in the YHA newsletter. We weren't expecting much, but we got replies and met up with a few people in the Old Boars Head in Middleton. Apart from the four of us, regular members were Jack and Margaret, Dave, and Bill, who became the club secretary. Things moved on quickly, and we soon started to set up walking trips. We spent one weekend in Wasdale walking and climbing. We stayed on the Wasdale Head campsite and spent the obligatory two nights drinking in the Wasdale Head. On the Saturday night, staggering back to our camp, I tripped and fell into the roadside hedge. When I picked myself up, I had one of my most amazing experiences – my hands were glowing in the darkness. It took me a minute to realise what was going on. My hands were covered in glow worms! We also had great a trip to Malham, where we had a minibus full, with a canoe on the roof, and camped near Malham Cove. So, the club was in full swing and going from strength to strength.

At this juncture, I need to mention that when I was 16, I got a Saturday Job working in Boots at the Arndale Centre in Middleton. It was a largish store on two floors. The hours were 9 am to 6 pm, the pay was just over £7 quid, and luckily, the manager was a fairly decent bloke. I started work in the stock room working with a lad called K[72]. Our job was to keep the stock sorted and deal with deliveries. The good news was that by about 3 pm, it had gone quiet, so we used to play footy in the back yard. I had a few escapades while I was there, including a time when a dog pooped on the shop floor and the manager told me to clean it up and I refused, so he had to do it himself. Nowadays, you would probably be sacked! One day, K and I were given the task of carrying the store takings to the local bank. I can remember being nervous about this. It was a bag containing thousands of pounds in cash, but it was also an excuse to bunk off for a bit. It was all very

---

[72] I'm sure his name began with a K. Was it Kevin or Keith? I'm afraid I can't remember the names of any of the staff there.

1970s. Can you imagine that happening now? Anyway, we survived the experience and no money was stolen.

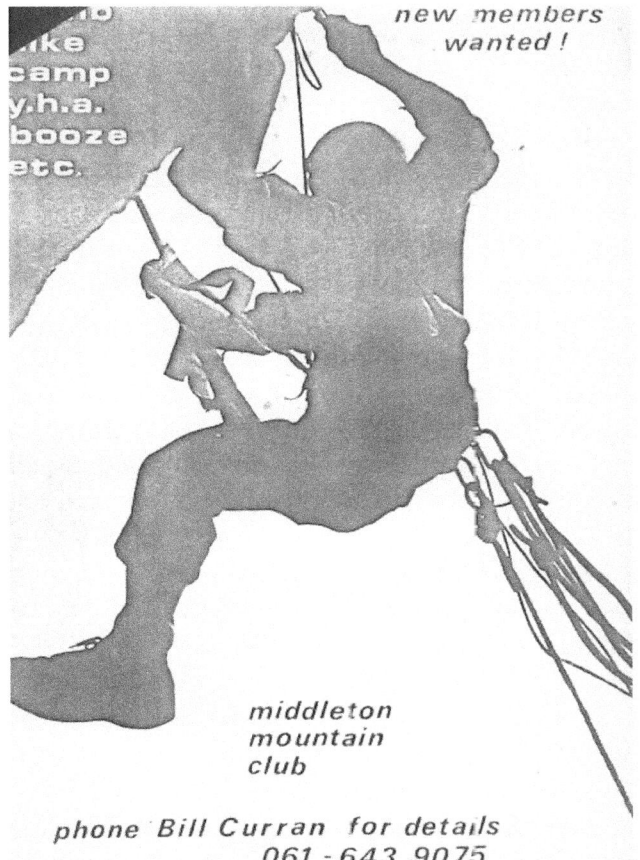

Middleton Mountain Club flyer

Later on, I got a 'promotion' and started working in the main store. There was some shelf filling to do, which I didn't mind, and also some cleaning, but in the afternoon, I was able to take charge of the record section upstairs! It was nirvana for me. Not only could I play records of my choice but I could also buy them at staff discount. My record collection soon expanded, and I was able to order some records that I wanted. Perfect! The manager knew I was doing A levels, and he offered to help me get a place at Nottingham University, sponsored by Boots, to study pharmacy. This didn't appeal at the time because

I wanted to be a biologist. With the advantage of hindsight, it might have been much better if I'd take up his offer!

The 1970s were a fractious decade, a time of crises and industrial strife. In 1971, USA, under President Nixon, ditched the Bretton Woods agreement of 1944, which regulated currencies globally, and this was the start of many economic problems, and global instability. After the disaster of the Tories winning the 1970 general election, Anthony Barber, the Tory Chancellor, introduced policies that led to inflation, the infamous 'Barber Boom', and successful industrial action by the Miners in 1972 and 1974[73]. During the 1974 strike, there were power cuts and the government was forced to introduce the infamous Three Day Week. This, in turn, led the Conservative Prime Minister Edward Heath to call a general election in February 1974 on "Who governs Britain?". The answer he got was "Not you", and he had to resign after the Tories lost their majority. Harold Wilson became Prime Minister with a minority government. He subsequently held another general election in October 1974 and emerged with a small majority.

As if this wasn't enough, there was also the 'OPEC[74] oil crisis' in 1973. This was an oil embargo on a number of countries, including UK and USA, and lasted from October 1973 to March 1974. By the end of the embargo, the price of oil had risen nearly 300%! This of course led to high inflation, which plagued UK for most of the rest of the decade, leading to more industrial action as workers' wages shrank in value. Then in 1975, we had the European Communities membership referendum, which was the first time I was able to vote. I voted to be 'in'. Sixty-seven percent of people voted in favour of remaining in the 'Common Market', as it was called then, which Heath had taken us into two and a half years earlier. Rampant inflation and industrial action meant that while working at Boots, I got a number of pay rises during the two years I was there, even though I never had to go on strike – something you can't imagine happening nowadays. That whole decade is beautifully covered by E. P. Thompson in his book Writing by Candlelight – definitely recommended reading – which is something many of us had to do during power cuts of

---

[73] The Tories never forgot or forgave this victory and they were determined to defeat the Miners when they went on strike again in 1984.

[74] The Organisation of the Petroleum Exporting Countries which included Venezuela, Saudi Arabia and Iran.

the power workers' strike in 1970! Get hold of this book if you want to know more about this period.

The 1960s and 70s were also a time of fighting for equality and racial justice, leading to the founding of the Civil Rights movement in USA with fighters like Martin Luther King and Malcolm X. Also in USA, the Stonewall riots, which took place in 1969 after a police raid on the Stonewall Inn in New York, began a fight for gay rights, which eventually helped to bring about real positive change Feminism was also on the rise with the Women's Liberation Movement and the founding of the magazine Spare Rib and the publisher Virago by Carmen Callil in 1973 in UK. Despite the economic turmoil, there was a sense of real optimism and energy for change.

Of course, these socially liberal revolutions, including a more liberal attitude to sex, provoked a backlash and conservatives like Mary Whitehouse who led attacks on the 'permissive society'. She founded the National Viewers and Listeners Association and attacked the BBC for the use of bad language and sex and violence on television.

Probably, the biggest horror of the 1960s and 70s was the Vietnam war. It actually began in the 1950s in the French colony of Indochina. The French withdrew from the region in 1954 after being defeated by the revolutionary movement, the Viet Minh. Then the Americans got involved in what was really a cold war era proxy war with China and the Soviet Union. The conflict escalated under John F Kennedy after he increased American military involvement in 1964. The Americans eventually withdrew, defeated, in 1973. The Vietnam war was covered on the TV news pretty much every night during my childhood with horrific scenes of fighting, bodies, and carpet bombing[75]. It was hard to watch, but most people did.

Another atrocity of the 1970s occurred in Northern Ireland (NI) and became known as 'The Troubles'. It started with a civil rights campaign and protests in the late 1960s. The Irish nationalist community suffered discrimination, and elections were gerrymandered to give the unionists an electoral majority in places like Derry. The NI government tried to suppress the protests using the Royal Ulster Constabulary (RUC). The RUC were overwhelmingly protestant and

---

[75] The scenes were similar to those of the wars in Iraq and Ukraine but if anything more graphic, and no trigger warnings then.

were accused of sectarianism and police brutality. As the violence escalated, paramilitary organisations such as the republican Provisional IRA and the unionist Ulster Volunteer Force (UVF) became involved. The British government sent in the army, and on 30 January 1972, 13 unarmed men were shot dead by the British soldiers during a rally, an incident which became known as Bloody Sunday. The conflict lasted for 30 years and is usually deemed to have ended with the Good Friday agreement of 1998. Like the war in Vietnam, every evening, we witnessed the violence and strife of the conflict on TV.

In the 1970s, there was a resurgence in racist nationalism and the National Front held a number of marches. In response, Rock Against Racism and the Anti-Nazi League were set up. I supported both of these groups and attended the great gig in Victoria Park (see below). Apart from that, I wasn't very active in politics. I supported the striking workers in their industrial action and considered joining the Labour Party but decided that the Party of Wilson and Benn was too right wing for me! I wanted fundamental change not tinkering, and I still do!

I was also a keen environmentalist in my teens, something I have stuck to all of my life. I followed developments in solar power and wind turbines. I also had an interest in the idea of self-sufficiency, something I shared with my Dad. We were inspired by the British pioneer John Seymour. I still have two of his classic books from that period – The Fat of the Land and The Complete Book of Self Sufficiency – which I would highly recommend if you are interested. Alas, I never achieved the dream.

The 1970s ended almost as badly as they had started with the winter of discontent – November 1978 to February 1979. It was triggered, in part, by a 5% pay rise cap introduced by James Callaghan's Labour government. Many public and private sector unions were engaged in strike action for better pay, and the streets were strewn with rubbish from unemptied bins. Callaghan's denial that there was chaos-led The Sun's famous "Crisis? What Crisis?" headline. After that, Labour were in trouble and Margaret Thatcher was elected as Conservative PM later that year. Many people seem to have forgotten that her government was incredibly unpopular and that her premiership was only saved by the Falklands war in 1982.

Teenage Angst

In Easter 1975, MMC planned a trip to Edale, camping, walking, and climbing. I was really looking forward to it, but disaster struck. The manager at Boots wouldn't give me the Saturday off! I was tempted to quit, but I needed that job, and I wanted to be able to work during the summer holidays to save up for university. Luckily, a couple of the guys in MMC offered to pick me up on Sunday morning and drive me over to Edale, so it wouldn't be a wasted weekend.

That night, I got home from work, packed my bags, and got an early night. In the middle of the might, my sleep was interrupted by a strange and vivid dream. I dreamt I was in the Lake District walking up Pillar. When I reached the summit, I met Dave, who was waiting to speak to me. We had a conversation in which he told me he was dead! I woke up in shock and a cold sweat and looked at the alarm clock. It was four o'clock in the morning. I managed to go back into a fitful sleep, and by the time I awoke, it was t me to get up and get going.

After breakfast, I walked down Mainway to Manchester New Road to meet the guys in my boots and walking gear. I was on time and only had to wait about 5 minutes for their car to arrive. As they pulled up, I sensed something was wrong; they weren't wearing any walking gear. They wound down the window and said "get in". What was going on? The guy in the passenger seat turned round and said "I'm sorry to have to tell you this but Dave is dead". Dead? How could that be possible? "He was killed yesterday in a climbing accident". I was stunned. I couldn't believe it. They drove me home in complete silence. I thanked them and went indoors to tell my Mum and Dad.

Dave had been rock-climbing on a crag on Kinder Scout. The guy leading the ascent who was above him had pulled himself up on a rock boulder, and the boulder came away from the rock face. The guy fell and the boulder hit Dave, kil ing him instantly. The guy who fell suffered serious injuries and ended up in hospital. Thankfully, he recovered. So that was it, a cruel accident. I couldn't believe it. I had lost my best friend. I spent the rest of the day in shock. Phone calls were made. I went to the funeral. I lent Dave's mum some photos I had taken of him, and, foolishly, I never asked to get any back. So I no longer have a photo of his face, only cne picture of him from the back, on the summit of Y Garn, surveying the snowy mountains in the Idwal valley on that glorious weekend we had together.

Not long after Dave died, a friend called Roger came round to visit me and offer his condolences. It was kind of him, but I made a big mistake. He offered me a cigarette, and I thought "Why the hell not". I was in the mood for it. That was the start of me smoking after having avoided it through my teens – in part due to my experience in Anglesey. I graduated to roll-ups and then continued smoking for 30 years!

It's difficult for me to follow on from that, but I guess now it's time for something a lot easier and much less painful to relate – my only claim to fame. But it's not a bad one. In the Sixth Form at Hulme, I got invited to a party by a friend John, who lived in Saddleworth. His dad was a bit of a local celebrity – a cartoonist for the Oldham Chronicle. How I got to the party I'm not sure, but I must have scrounged a lift off someone. It was the usual thing, lots of teenagers, loud music, beers, and the smell of fags. No doubt Dark Side of the Moon by Pink Floyd was played at some point, as it was at every party in those days. Towards the end of the night, I managed to get a smooching session with an older girl who I later found out was John's sister Ann. I had snogged John's sister - the future Deidre Barlow![76]

I need to mention some of my escapades with my school friends Barry and Steve. Steve lived in Chadderton and Barry in Oldham, so I used to meet up with them in Oldham on a Saturday night, and we do a pub crawl, playing pool and listening to our favourites on the juke box. Pubs shut at 11 pm in those days, and the last bus[77] back was at 10:30. Guess what? I regularly missed the last bus! I used to walk back home in the dark, pissed, down Oldham Road. I couldn't afford a taxi. Fortunately for me, it was downhill nearly all the way. Occasionally, I was lucky enough to be able to bunk over at Barry's place, where we used to listen to Todd Rundgren albums and smoke spliffs.

We had a great night when we went over to stay with a school-friend John. His parents were hippies and lived near Littleborough. John was a really talented guy but, as I recall, not much interested in academia. We sat under the stars on a warm sunny night by a campfire and smoked spliffs while John played guitar. What a wonderful evening!

---

[76] She wasn't Deidre then of course but she went on to be one of the big stars of Coronation Street.
[77] Was it the no. 59? That's my recollection.

Now I need to mention the strip club wild night out in Manchester. Barry had a friend whose name I forget. Let's call him 'S'. He had a car, and one Saturday night, he picked us all up and drove us out to Manchester for a night on the town. This was luxury for me. Getting drunk and chauffeured was ideal! S had very definite ideas about where he wanted to go, so we tagged along. The first stop was Canal Street. Then, as now, it was the gay part of town, but in those days, it was pretty seedy. We went to the Queens Hotel on the corner, got some beers, and watched an oldish guy in drag trying a Shirley Bassey impression – a whole new experience for me. The next stop was Rembrandts. Now, my recollection is that had sprung doors like a wild west saloon. We pushed to doors open to a noisy bar full of guys in leather who looked like the Village People, and one or two people who might have been women. As we entered, the whole place went silent and everybody turned to look at us. We bottled it, walking out backwards, a fast exit!

The highlight of the night for S was the strip club. He's been talking about it all the way down in the car. He told us that if you sat on the front row, the stripper would come down from the stage and put her knickers on your head. We looked at each other and grinned but said nothing. The strip club was in a back alley in an even seedier part of town, in what looked like an old mill. You went in and up some stairs. At the top was a very large guy who demanded five pounds entry. Five pounds! I didn't have that on me. Fortunately, Barry was able to cover me. We entered a large, gloomy room with a bar near the door and a stage at the far end. The room was filled with men in dirty Macs – I kid you not! The bar served expensive watered-down Double Diamond. We got our drinks while S scuttled down to the front row as we expected, along with the dirty mac brigade, and we remained at the back. After a short pause, the curtains opened, the music started, and the stripper came on. She did a fairly short act, came down from the stage, and placed her knickers on the head of an old guy who sat next to S! Very loud guffaws came from where we were sitting on the back row. That was the grand finale of our seedy night out!

I need to mention three other adventures with Barry and Steve, even though, strictly speaking, they are outside the scope of this book, which ends with me leaving home in 1975 to go to university.

The first was a trip in 1976 at the end of my first year at university with Steve to see the Rolling Stones at Knebworth. We hitched down together and were lucky enough to get a lift in a transit van with some hippies who were going there. We got there late at night and kipped in the van. We were up at sunrise and into the gig to get some food and pick a prime spot. We hung around for hours, and it was a warm, sunny day. On the bill were Lynyrd Skynyrd, who I wasn't mad about, but their rendition of Freebird went down very well. The gig was marred by what seemed interminable delays between sets, and eventually, 10cc came on and did a great set.

After another long delay, the Rolling Stones finally came on to rapturous applause! I think they came on at about midnight. But what a gig! They were superb! Disaster struck, though after about four songs when I had just had to go for a piss. I was in pain and about to burst. I'd thought about doing it there, but it would have been impossible not to pee on someone in that tightly packed crowd. "Sorry Steve I've got to go". We worked our way slowly back through the crowd of over 100,000 ecstatic fans. I had a pee in a foul pit. The disappointment of not being close to the stage was ameliorated by the excellent music and the large b&w screens we could watch them play on. They finished at about 2 pm. I can't recall where we crashed, but it was a great day and one I'll always remember.

The second was another great gig, this time in Newcastle, where Barry was at university. We went to see Television and Blondie at The City Hall on 23 May 1977, two of my favourite all time bands. I loved Television's first album Marquee Moon, great songs and superb guitar playing from Tom Verlaine, and who could resist Debbie Harry? It was an epic night with only one drawback – the sound was way too loud. I staggered out practically stone deaf, and my ears were still ringing the next day. Fabulous stuff though. I wouldn't have missed it for the world.

The other was when I hitched down to London with Barry to see The Clash play at the Victoria Park in Hackney on 30 April 1978. It was a Rock Against Racism gig. We managed to catch the march and walked from central London to the park. Also on the set list were Steel Pulse, X-Ray Spex – "Oh bondage up yours!", The Tom Robinson Band – "Sing if you're glad to Be gay", and Patrick Fitzgerald. We were lucky with the weather which was fine, and we had no trouble in our Levi denims keeping warm in the crowd. The bands were all very good, but when The Clash came on, the place exploded! Thousands of people began pogoing in unison! We were fairly near to the front, and there was no choice but to go with the flow. We pogoed because we had to, pretty bit scary actually, but I don't think anyone was injured. The Clash were by then my favourite band, and I loved every second of that set! Another classic gig and a great day out! No idea how we got home though.

Television and Blondie in Newcastle

Something else I want to add to this tale that should really be outside the scope of this book is the mysterious incident in the bathroom in the night-time, if only because it was so bizarre. In 1982, I was living in Lancaster after leaving the university. I lived in a shared house on South Road. I had a basement room[78]. It was gloomy but had the advantage of being next to the toilet, bathroom, and kitchen. One Saturday evening, while it was still light, I decided to have a bath before going out. I ran the bath and was lying there having a good soak when something very strange happened – smoke began to flow under the bathroom door! I could hardly believe it, but the room was rapidly filling with smoke, so I jumped out of the bath and grabbed a towel. The hallway outside the bathroom was full of smoke, and I began to cough. The house was on fire! I ran through the kitchen and out into the back garden wrapped in a towel. Then I heard the sound of a fire engine. I looked up at the house, expecting to see flames coming out of the windows, but there was nothing. What was happening? Gradually, it dawned on me that the firefighters were next door – not at our house. I later discovered that the thick smoke had come from a chip pan fire in the kitchen of the house next to ours.

Six months later, I was at Essex University studying biology and staying in a student flat in Avon Way. It was Saturday night, and the three guys I shared the flat with were already out. I decided to have a bath before going down to the bar. I ran the bath and was lying there once again having good soak when – you've guessed it – smoke began to come under the bathroom door. This can't be happening! But it was! Once again, I grabbed my towel and made a rapid exit only to discover the flat was full of smoke! I legged it out of the flat door which closed shut behind me.

I was locked out, and I was in a stairwell between the flats. I immediately had a problem; it was November and icy cold! If I didn't burn, I might well freeze. What to do? I banged on the flat door opposite, and to my relief, someone was in and opened it. But er…. it was a women's flat and the arrival of a half naked wet man in a towel was a bit of a shock to them. I can't say I was bothered; it was a relief to be out of the cold and my teeth were still chattering. Despite some

---

[78] I've lived in many shared houses and I had the bad habit of always being the last in and getting the least desirable room, usually the box room!

embarrassment, the ladies rose to the occasion, took pity on me, and found me another big towel and a jumper that fitted and made me a cup of tea. They looked after me. Then we heard the fire engine. I imagine you've already guessed the end of this tale. Later that evening, we found out that the smoke was caused by a chip pan fire in the flat below mine. How I managed to regain entry to the flat is a story in itself, but I'll spare you the details. I'm happy to say that I did manage to get to the bar before closing time and had a few well-earned pints. Since then, I can assure you I have avoided chip pans but not baths!

So how does this story of mine really end? It ends with me getting what I wanted – a place at university. But even that wasn't simple. I took my A levels in 1975 not long after Dave died, and, as I mentioned earlier, I cocked them up. I'm not using his death as an excuse, but it certainly didn't help. Sitting down at the dining room table, opening the envelope, and reading the results was one of the saddest things I've ever experienced.

Initially, I had applied to do medicine and got an offer of three Bs from Manchester University. I ended up with a BCD, getting an O level pass in Physics! What hurt most was the C in chemistry, probably my best subject, in which I got an A in the mocks. I made my first ever blunder in an exam by misreading the paper and trying to answer four questions in a section where I only needed to answer one of them! The B in biology was straightforward thankfully.

So, now it was going through the university clearing system. I was offered a place at Lancaster university to study biochemistry, something which really interested me. I had been inspired by scientists like Watson and Crick and Linus Pauling and wanted to do research and complete a PhD. At least I had achieved my aim of successfully getting into university. I was leaving home to do what I'd wanted for years, and I was happy about that. I couldn't wait to get there. My parents were pleased for me but sad to see me go. So I packed up my bags, and my Mum and Dad drove me up to Lonsdale College. I even arrived a day early. A new life was beginning, and one I was really looking forward to! One thing that is worth mentioning is that I got a student grant and didn't have to pay any fees. I can remember that my grant amounted to £14 per week and my rent was £7 a week. And yes, you could survive on seven quid and even have some beers!

How to Build a Snowman and Other Stories

Ready to go to university?

Chapter 10
AFTERWORD

So what was it really like growing up in the 1960s and 70s? On the whole, it was pretty good. I was lucky enough to have parents who loved me, and we lived in a 'modern' house. The 1960s were seen as a time of optimism and innovation and the 1970s a time of strife, but it was much more complicated than that. One of the key factors about living in those times in UK was that many more things were affordable. If you had a reasonable salary, and many people did, you could afford to buy a house. People who couldn't had the security of council housing to fall back on. Many people had permanent jobs – jobs for life if they wanted them, and they had decent final salary pensions. You could access higher education and improve yourself and your life chances without being burdened with debt. Many of these advantages have been lost after forty of years of neoliberalism that has increased insecurity and poverty, and damaged public services. There were poor people in those days but no foodbanks or warm banks which millions need in the 2020s. Yes, UK was a more racist, sexist, and homophobic society then, and things have improved since, but we weren't plagued by culture wars and bullshit about wokeness, and transphobia, not that racism, homophobia, and sexism has been eradicated by any means.

We didn't have computers and the Internet, but that had its advantages. You had to make the effort to arrange to meet up and socialise with people, not that it doesn't happen now, but it happened then without being glued to a smartphone or being dependent on apps, and we still managed perfectly well. Millions of people weren't exposed to bizarre conspiracy theories on social media platforms owned by billionaires and surrounded by thousands of streaming services. Kids played out in the street, without their parents worrying about them being molested or abducted, instead of being ensconced in bedrooms with their tablets. People took the time to write letters to friends, family, and lovers, much more fulfilling than a text! Perhaps 'less is more' would be an appropriate description. And we weren't surrounded by plastic. As I've already mentioned, milk was delivered in glass bottles by an electric milk float, soft drinks were in glass bottles, and there was a deposit on a beer bottle so that you returned them to the offy – all much better for the environment. Some things have improved for sure, but I can't help thinking the power of oligarchs, markets, and corporations, and the growing corruption of democracy is leading us into a dark place driven by our damaging dependence on fossil fuels. This isn't about some sort of nostalgia for the past; it's about the fact that in some respects we've gone backwards since those days.

The future for young people looks bleak, and the biodiversity of the Earth looks grim. Not only that, but those forty odd years of neoliberalism – starting with Thatcher and Reagan in the 1980s – have done huge damage to the fabric of our society with public services being privatised, wages for workers lowered, and a very real threat to the future of the NHS. Despite this, I remain fairly optimistic about the future. What other choice is there!

But what happened to me next? Quite a lot! Much of the stuff I've written here happened about fifty years ago. My stay at Lancaster University wasn't a success, and I had a hard time after leaving at the end of my first year. I suffered from depression for about 6 months afterwards – saved by Dr Leveson! I met some good people at Lancaster University including my friends Bob, Liz, and Martin, who I still see. I managed to get back into university, and I went on to get a good degree in biology at Essex University. I had a fantastic time there after a number of years of working in fairly low paid jobs in Lancaster. After completing my degree, I decided I needed a trade after being skint for so long so I did a PGCE in Nottingham and ended up teaching biology and chemistry for four years at a comprehensive in London. My time in London is a tale in itself.

I had a very difficult time with the deaths of my parents. My mother died when she was fifty, from pneumonia, while I was on holiday in the Yorkshire Dales (no mobile phones then). I didn't find out until I got back home. She was failed by the NHS, which made me angry. Thirty years later, my father died of a heart attack while he was on holiday in Spain with my stepmother Carol. He died in his sleep after enjoying the night before in a bar. He was nearly eighty. It took us two weeks for us to get him repatriated. So, I missed the deaths of both my parents, and I wasn't able to say goodbye to either of them. I have always regretted that.

I was, and still am, a keen environmentalist, so after doing a Masters at Manchester University in Pollution and Environmental Control,

Afterword

I returned to living in Manchester and then worked as an environmental regulator, specialising in resource efficiency and recycling, for nearly twenty five years. I've had many ups and downs, but all in all, I've had a pretty good life. I even eventually managed to give up cigarettes! I'm still politically active and write for a socialist magazine and have my own blog. My main concern is the climate crisis we are facing and the lack of action by governments to reduce greenhouse gas emissions. As I write this, CoP 27 is due to take place in Egypt soon and the new PM Rishi Sunak can't even be bothered to attend[79].

If you want to find out more about the climate crisis and the problems of neoliberalism, especially around the lies we are told by the media and politicians about government funding, taxes, and debt, I recommend you read the books below. We need to work together, build solidarity and mutual aid, organise ourselves, and fight for a better future!

But first a bit of indulgence. Here are some of my favourite books and albums from that time, which I enjoyed and which influenced me, in no particular order:

Albums:

- Revolver - The Beatles
- The Clash - The Clash
- What's Going On - Marvin Gaye
- Pet Sounds - The Beach Boys
- Innervisions - Stevie Wonder
- Visions of the Emerald Beyond - Mahavishnu Orchestra
- Caravanserai - Sanatana
- Natty Dread - Bob Marley
- Ziggy Stardust - David Bowie
- Kind of Blue - Miles Davis

Books:

- The Weirdstone of Brisingamen - Alan Garner
- The History of Western Philosophy - Bertrand Russell

---

[79] Of course, as I suspected, he changed his mind shortly after I wrote this.

- Anarchism - George Woodcock
- Homage to Catalonia - George Orwell
- On The Road - Jack Kerouac
- The Grapes of Wrath - John Steinbeck
- The Age of Reason - John Paul Sartre
- The Fat of the Land - John Seymour
- The Adventures of Sherlock Holmes - Arthur Conan Doyle
- The Catcher in the Rye - JD Salinger

And recommended reading for our times:

- The Climate Wars - Michael E Mann
- The Deficit Myth - Stephanie Kelton
- America: The Farewell Tour - Chris Hedges
- Less is More - Jason Hickel
- The Global Minotaur - Yanis Varoufakis
- The Joy of Tax - Richard J Murphy
- The Book of Trespass - Nick Hayes
- From What Is To What If - Rob Hopkins
- The Persuaders - Anand Giridharadas
- The Lost Rainforests of Britain - Guy Shrubsole

I want to finish with a quote from Bob Dylan – "The Times They Are A-Changin":

The line it is drawn
The curse it is cast
The slow one now
Will later be fast
As the present now
Will later be past
The order is rapidly fadin'
And the first one now
Will later be last
For the times they are a-changin'

www.ingramcontent.com/pod-product-compliance
Ingram Content Group UK Ltd.
Pitfield, Milton Keynes, MK11 3LW, UK
UKHW020628120225
4558UKWH00015B/383